BACK TO
SANITY

BACK TO
SANITY

HEALING THE MADNESS OF OUR MINDS

STEVE TAYLOR

HAY HOUSE

Australia • Canada • Hong Kong • India
South Africa • United Kingdom • United States

First published and distributed in the United Kingdom by:
Hay House UK Ltd, 292B Kensal Rd, London W10 5BE. Tel.: (44) 20 8962 1230;
Fax: (44) 20 8962 1239. www.hayhouse.co.uk

Published and distributed in the United States of America by:
Hay House, Inc., PO Box 5100, Carlsbad, CA 92018-5100. Tel.: (1) 760 431 7695
or (800) 654 5126; Fax: (1) 760 431 6948 or (800) 650 5115.
www.hayhouse.com

Published and distributed in Australia by:
Hay House Australia Ltd, 18/36 Ralph St, Alexandria NSW 2015.
Tel.: (61) 2 9669 4299; Fax: (61) 2 9669 4144. www.hayhouse.com.au

Published and distributed in the Republic of South Africa by:
Hay House SA (Pty), Ltd, PO Box 990, Witkoppen 2068.
Tel./Fax: (27) 11 467 8904. www.hayhouse.co.za

Published and distributed in India by:
Hay House Publishers India, Muskaan Complex, Plot No.3, B-2, Vasant Kunj,
New Delhi – 110 070. Tel.: (91) 11 4176 1620; Fax: (91) 11 4176 1630.
www.hayhouse.co.in

Distributed in Canada by:
Raincoast, 9050 Shaughnessy St, Vancouver, BC V6P 6E5.
Tel.: (1) 604 323 7100; Fax: (1) 604 323 2600

Text © Steve Taylor, 2012

The moral rights of the author have been asserted.

The information given in this book should not be treated as a substitute for
professional medical advice; always consult a medical practitioner. Any use
of information in this book is at the reader's discretion and risk. Neither the
author nor the publisher can be held responsible for any loss, claim or damage
arising out of the use, or misuse, or the suggestions made or the failure to take
medical advice.

A catalogue record for this book is available from the British Library.

ISBN 978-1-84850-547-6

Printed and bound in Great Britain by TJ International, Padstow, Cornwall

To Bill,
who may live to see
a saner world.

Contents

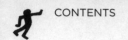

Introduction

Since Europeans began exploring and colonizing the world in the sixteenth century, they have curiously observed 'indigenous' peoples and written accounts of their cultures. Modern anthropologists still frequently travel to remote corners of the world to observe and document tribes that haven't yet been touched by globalization, and still follow traditional lifestyles.

But what about the other way round? What have indigenous peoples made of the 'developed' peoples who have studied them, and whose culture has conquered theirs? Or to put it more abstractly, if a member of a remote tribe wrote an anthropological study of us, what would it say?

In 1932, the psychologist Carl Jung met Native American Chief Mountain Lake in New Mexico. When Jung asked him what he thought of the European people who had conquered his country, he gave a damning assessment: 'The whites always want something. They are always uneasy and restless. We do not know what they want. We do not understand them. We think that they are all mad.'[1]

Other indigenous peoples have shared Mountain Lake's bemusement. Many believed that the Europeans' lust for possessions was a kind of madness. As the Sioux chief Sitting

Bull said: 'The love of possession is a disease with them... They claim this mother of ours, the Earth, for their own and fence their neighbors away.'[2]

In a similar way, many were shocked by the Europeans' lack of connection to – and reverence for – nature. As one of the most acute observers of the differences between the European and Indian worldviews, Chief Luther Standing Bear, wrote:

> *Indian faith sought the harmony of man with his surroundings; the other sought the dominance of surroundings... For [the Indian] the world was full of beauty, for [the white man] it was a place of sin and ugliness to be endured until he went to another world.*[3]

In other words, indigenous peoples seem to think that there is something wrong with us, even that we are mad. An indigenous anthropologist who studied our history would find a massive amount of further evidence for this too: thousands of years of constant warfare, massive inequalities of wealth and power, the brutal oppression of women, of other classes and castes, endless brutality, violence, and greed – and then, in recent decades, the suicidal destruction of our planet's life support systems. He or she would also look at the massive inequalities that blight the world today, where the three richest people in the world are wealthier than the 48 poorest countries combined, and where almost 800 million people are malnourished while millions of others are obese because they have too much food.[4]

What could be more insane than this?

Our psychological disorder

This book is my attempt to understand this human madness. Why do we find it impossible to live in harmony with each other, with the natural world, or even with our own selves? Why is human history an endless, depressing saga of warfare, conflict, and oppression? Why do we seem impelled to destroy our environment, and hence ourselves as a species? Or, on a more psychological level, why do we suffer from the constant restlessness and unease of which Mountain Lake spoke? Why is it that many of us are driven to accumulate more and more wealth, status, and success, without any evidence that they provide us with contentment and fulfillment? Why, when we achieve our goals, do we often only feel a short period of satisfaction, before restlessness emerges again, filling us with a desire to achieve even more?

Our basic problem, I suggest in this book, is that there really is something wrong with our minds. We suffer from a basic psychological disorder that is the source of our dysfunctional behavior, both as individuals and as a species. We're all slightly mad – but because the madness is so intrinsic to us, we're not aware of it. I call this disorder 'humania', as in 'human madness.' (I sometimes refer to it as 'ego-madness' too, since – as we'll see later – the disorder is the result of the malfunctioning and the mal-development of the ego. By the ego I mean our sense of being an 'I' within our own mental space, the 'self-system' that gives us a sense of being an individual, with our thoughts and experiences.)

The Diagnostic and Statistical Manual of Mental Disorders, or *DSM* – the standard manual used by American psychiatrists – defines a psychological or mental disorder as a 'clinically significant behavioral or psychological syndrome or pattern [which] is associated with present distress... or with a significant increased risk of suffering.'[5]

Humania is too omnipresent and taken for granted to be seen as clinically significant, but it's certainly the cause of distress and suffering. It means that the normal state of our minds is one of discord. The first noble truth of Buddhism is that 'life is suffering,' and this suffering begins in our minds. This inner suffering – or psychological discord, as I refer to it – is so normal to us that we don't realize it's there, like a background noise you're so accustomed to that you don't hear anymore. But it has massive consequences. It means that we have to keep our attention focused outside ourselves, and fill our lives with constant activity and distraction, like addicts needing a constant supply of a drug. It makes it impossible for us to find contentment. It causes discord in our relationships. It impels us to search for wellbeing and fulfillment outside ourselves, in wealth, success, and power. It's even responsible – for reasons that I'll explain later – for much of the conflict, oppression, and brutality that fill human history.

But despite its devastating effects, humania is neither deep-rooted nor permanent. In fact it only exists on a superficial layer of the mind. All of us regularly have moments when our normal psychological discord fades away and we experience a sense of ease, wellbeing and harmony. In these moments we're free of the pressure to keep busy, and the need for stimulation and acquisition – we rest at ease within ourselves and within the present moment.

These moments of 'harmony of being' – as I refer to them – usually happen when we're quiet and relaxed, and there's stillness around us: for example, when we're walking through the countryside, working quietly with our hands, listening to or playing music, after meditation, yoga or sex. The normal incessant chattering of our minds fades away and, rather than feeling separate, we feel a natural flow of connection between ourselves and our surroundings or other people. In these moments, we become – temporarily, at least – sane.

This harmony and sanity are *always* inside us, in the same way that the deep stillness of the sea is always beneath the roar of the waves. The problem is that the superficial discord of our minds denies us access to it. Rather than going into ourselves and experiencing the harmony of our essential being, we are pushed out of ourselves, into distractions and activity, and so unable to live in the present and unable to find contentment.

The aims of this book

This book has two aims. First, we're going to examine our psychological disorder, to investigate its characteristics and understand its causes, in much the same way a doctor might examine and diagnose an illness. We're going to look at the different types of insane behavior that characterize us as human beings: first, our pathological behavior as individuals, such as constant activity and distraction, materialism and status-seeking; and then our collective pathological behavior, such as warfare, environmental destruction and dogmatic religion. Then we're going to examine how humania gives rise to these behaviors. This section of the book may sometimes be slightly bleak, but bear in mind that, in order to treat and heal an illness, it's necessary to examine it in as much detail as possible.

This healing is the second aim of the book. In the last four chapters, we're going to examine how we can transcend our psychological discord. I'll suggest certain practices and ways of living – as well as a number of practical exercises – that will help to heal our disordered minds, and create a more harmonious inner state, so that we can begin to live inside ourselves, and in the present, and so that we can attain a state of real sanity.

So if happiness and fulfillment are eluding you, if you feel 'messed up' in some way, plagued by worries, poisoned by bitterness and regret; if you feel that life is so full of suffering that (as a friend of mine said to me recently) you wouldn't have asked to be born – you can take some consolation from the fact that these are largely just the symptoms of a psychological condition; and that this condition can be healed.

However, this isn't just about improving our lives or making us more contented as individuals. Ultimately, our madness makes it impossible for us to live in an appropriate and sustainable way on our planet. As many indigenous people have recognized, the end point of our chronic restlessness and rampant materialism is self-destruction. We will only be able to live in harmony with our planet, other species and with each other when we are able to live in harmony with ourselves.

PART I

THE MADNESS OF HUMAN BEINGS

CHAPTER 1

The Madness of Living Outside Ourselves

In some ways, those of us who live in the world's richer countries – in Europe and North America, for instance – are the luckiest human beings who have ever lived. Until just a few generations ago, human beings' average life expectancy was between 30 and 40. Almost a third of people died before reaching adulthood, and most of those who survived spent their lives in abject poverty, suffering – and dying – from cold, hunger, and a variety of illnesses and health problems that have now largely been eradicated: constant toothache (hence the nineteenth-century saying that 'a third of all human suffering is toothache'), scurvy, smallpox, tuberculosis, and so on. If your eyesight was poor you would spend your life with blurred vision, if you broke a limb you would be crippled for the rest of your life, and if your children contracted illnesses such as measles or tuberculosis, there was a good chance they would die.

But now, in the first decade of the twenty-first century, we are largely free from these problems. Our life expectancy has increased dramatically – until 80 in some countries – and most of us spend these extra decades in relative comfort, with heating in our homes, food in our cupboards, and access to amazingly effective medical care (at least in most European countries and Canada – unfortunately the USA still has some catching up to do in this regard).

It's even possible to say that we're the first *free* human beings. Most of us are free in a *material* sense – largely free from the physical battle to keep ourselves alive in the face of poverty and hunger. We're also free in a *social* sense – free in the sense that we're not chained to the social niche into which we were born. We don't have to spend our lives as peasants, hardly setting foot outside the village in which we were born; we have a large degree of social mobility. You could even say that we're free in an intellectual sense – whereas just a couple of centuries ago, education and knowledge were the privilege of a tiny minority, now they are available to most of us.

Surely we should be the happiest human beings who have ever lived? Surely we should be filled with joy, having gained the freedom, prosperity and health that our ancestors could only have dreamed of?

But it hasn't worked out like that, of course. In fact, it may very well be that we're *less* happy than our ancestors. Our freedom hasn't turned out to be the blessing it appeared. Rather than spending our extra decades in a state of joyful appreciation, many of us suffer from different forms of psychological malaise, such as depression, drug abuse or eating disorders, or else a general sense of anxiety, boredom or dissatisfaction, feeling as if something is somehow 'not quite right.' We seem to find our freedom a burden, and fill the leisure time we've been given with distractions like TV.

Famously, the psychologist Abraham Maslow showed that human needs make up a hierarchy. We have certain lower needs that need to be satisfied before we can move up to higher needs, i.e. we have to first satisfy our needs for food and shelter before we can start to think about satisfying our needs for love and self-esteem. However, there is also a negative side to this: once we've satisfied our basic physical needs, and move up to emotional and psychological ones, we're faced with psychological problems that weren't evident before. After being too preoccupied with survival to be aware of it, we encounter our psychological discord – and it's this that is the obstacle to our happiness.

It's as if we aren't able to live with ourselves. After spending centuries with our attention focused outside, now that we've turned inside and faced ourselves, a giant can of psychological worms has opened up.

The madness of distraction

You come home from work and open your front door. You've had a stressful day and the quietness and emptiness of your home seems somehow uncomfortable, so the first thing you do is switch on the radio. Then you make yourself a sandwich and sit down at the table. Even with the radio on, it feels as if there's something missing; it doesn't feel right to just sit there quietly eating, looking out at the street through the front window or at the lawn and shrubs through the back. You feel the urge to latch your attention on to something. There's an inner compulsion to *immerse your attention* in something. So you reach for a magazine and flick through it while you eat.

This urge to immerse our attention in external things is so instinctive that we're scarcely aware of it. Our attention is like a beam that always needs to be focused, attached to an external object. When it's loose and unfixed we feel uncomfortable. We feel a sense of lack, and so whenever our attention isn't occupied we're always scouring our surroundings for a possible 'attention hook' – a book, a newspaper, the TV, or the Internet.

Of course, often we experience this impulse to immerse our attention in a more overt way. You don't have enough money to go out in the evening, and so you're stuck at home feeling 'bored.' The idea of just moping around doing nothing in particular is unthinkable – that would just make you feel worse. By the end of the evening you'd be depressed. So you phone a friend for a chat and spend the rest of the evening watching a DVD and writing e-mails.

Or you're stuck on a long train journey – again, if you spent the time just staring out of the window with nothing in particular to do, you'd quickly start to feel uncomfortable. You might even start to worry about all kinds of things – that the train might be late, that your appointed meeting or conference will be a disaster, or more generally, that your relationship with your partner isn't what it should be. And so you make sure that you have enough activities and distractions to keep your mind occupied – you take a book, a newspaper, your laptop and your phone. The same goes for any situation where we have unfilled time in front of us – in the waiting room at the doctor or dentist, for example.

This is the reason why television is so popular. It's a very powerful 'attention hook', one of the best methods yet devised of keeping our attention focused outside ourselves. The average person in the USA watches TV for 28 hours a week – that's four hours a day outside themselves, immersed in the alternate realities of TV shows.

I'm not condemning TV outright – I know that a lot of shows are stimulating and amusing. Different people watch television for different reasons, and the same person may have different reasons for watching it at different times – to be informed or to be amused, for example. But there's no doubt that our main motivation for watching the box is to be taken out of ourselves.

Would we spend 30 hours a week immersed in the alternate reality of TV shows – and other alternate realities such as computer games – if we were truly contented with *this* reality?

The madness of doing

Many of us cherish a belief that there will be a time in our lives when we're finally able to sit back and relax. After working hard for years, we'll finally be happy with the level of success or wealth we've achieved, and feel entitled to rest and enjoy the fruits of our labor.

But again, it usually doesn't work that way. Most of us depend on activity in the same way that we depend on distractions such as TV. We use activity as another way of keep our attention focused outside ourselves.

Not long after leaving university, I took a temporary office job in the pensions department of an engineering firm. I did a number of dreary jobs around that time, but this was undoubtedly the dreariest. There was a small room in the office full of shelves packed with dozens of boxes of old pension forms – one for every person who had ever worked for the company. My task was to sort the forms into alphabetical order. There were thousands of them, and it took me two whole months.

One of my colleagues was a senior gentleman called Jimmy. When I asked him how long he'd worked there, he replied, 'Just a few months. I'm from a temping agency like you. I'm 66 – I retired from my proper job about a year ago. I was working in insurance.'

'So why did you start this job, just after retiring?'

'I didn't like having nothing to do,' he said. 'I like keeping myself busy.'

At the time I found this amazing. Why would someone who'd been set free from the routine drudgery of office work choose to go back to it, even though he didn't need the money? From my point of view, he could have been staying in bed late, reading books, going for walks in the countryside, taking up new hobbies. But he'd chosen to shut himself up in a stuffy office all day again.

A friend of mine recently told me about the experience of going back to live with his parents for a while, after splitting up with his partner. He was puzzled by the way that his mother would clean the house from top to bottom every single day, even though he couldn't see a speck of dust or dirt anywhere. Every carpet would be vacuumed again, every surface cleaned. It wasn't as though his mother was a housewife – she had a part-time job in the afternoons. But she didn't start work until midday, and liked to do the housework in the morning.

'Why are you doing the cleaning *again*?' he asked her one morning. 'It doesn't need doing again, surely?'

'Well *you* may like lazing around doing nothing,' she said, 'but I like keeping myself busy.'

I suspect that most of us have similar stories from our own lives. Most of us don't like being inactive, having empty periods of time in front of us, and so we like to find activities to fill them – some of which may be necessary, some not.

In this sense the term 'human being' is really a misnomer. One of the essential characteristics of human beings is that we find it impossible to *be*. If anything, we are human *doings*. An indigenous anthropologist would probably nickname us 'The creatures who can't do nothing' or perhaps 'The creatures who can't be alone with themselves.'

The dangers of doing nothing

I don't mean to disparage this impulse of ours to 'keep busy.' To a large extent we don't have any choice. We have to work hard to keep our attention focused outside ourselves, because when we don't, the consequences can be very negative.

I once knew a woman who found it impossible to be inactive for a moment. If she was left alone with herself for a few seconds with nowhere to focus her attention, she started to feel uneasy. She couldn't sit down. Even if the TV was on, she found it difficult to sit still. She never read books or newspapers and rarely listened to music. Those activities were too sedate for her; they didn't offer a strong enough focus for her attention.

However, she had quite a demanding job as a teacher, and during term time she didn't have so many problems. She didn't have much free time and managed to fill it fairly easily, mainly with shopping and socializing. Her real difficulties came in the school vacations, the 12 weeks a year when she wasn't busy. During these times she became desperate. You could see it in her eyes: a hint of panic and confusion, like a lost child. Activity was as vital to her as oxygen and without her eight hours of work each day she began to go to pieces. She tried to keep herself busy with shopping trips, days out, visiting friends, and so forth, but it was never enough. She became bad tempered and aggressive, and almost without fail, after a few days she became ill, usually with the flu or a throat infection.

It's as if there was a kind of monster inside her, causing discomfort and dread whenever she couldn't keep her attention focused outside herself.

This is an extreme example, but most of us share these characteristics to some degree, and suffer some negative effect when we're alone with ourselves for too long.

As a massive music fan – and former professional musician – I've always found it interesting that it's so common for pop musicians to fall prey to drug and drink problems and other psychological difficulties. Almost all of the major pop musicians of the last 40 years had drug or alcohol problems at some stage, some more serious than others: Elvis, Jimi Hendrix, Jim Morrison, Janis Joplin, Eric Clapton, Elton John, David Bowie, Kurt Cobain, Michael Jackson, Whitney Houston, Amy Winehouse and thousands of others not quite so famous. Some were lucky enough to recover from substance abuse, but many others died as a consequence. It's actually quite rare to find a pop musician – especially from the 1970s or 80s – who didn't have difficulties with cocaine, heroin, alcohol or another drug at some point.

There are a few possible reasons for this tendency toward abuse. Rock stars are used to having their egos continually affirmed by their fans, to thinking of themselves as special and important, and so an ego-boosting drug like cocaine appeals to them, because it sustains that sense of importance. Or from a different point of view, when ego-affirmation comes to an end, they may feel a sense of lack and turn to drugs to try to fill the void.

Pop musicians are also used to experiencing high levels of excitement when they play concerts, and the shift from this high-energy mode to everyday life may be too abrupt, and also leave them with a feeling of emptiness. They may take drugs to try to sustain that level of excitement and stimulation. And also, of course, money may be a factor: rock stars usually have massive amounts of ready cash to buy drugs. Or finally, for more introverted and sensitive people, a depressant like heroin might help to insulate them from the isolation and constant pressure of fame.

However, I believe that the main reason why so many pop musicians are prone to drug and alcohol abuse is very simple: they lead unstructured, inactive lives with a lot of traveling, hanging round, and empty time. Pop stars have much more leisure time than most of us. They don't have to get up to go to work in the mornings and put in eight hours at the office. This might seem like a blessing, but unless you're a self-reliant and self-motivated person, a large amount of free time and lack of structure can be disastrous. How does it feel to wake up every morning with no necessity to do anything and no planned activity ahead of you? What do you do for those months between tours or recording commitments, apart from hanging around and getting bored?

I remember this endless empty time from my four years as a musician – stuck inside a cramped, dirty van for hours at a time on the way to gigs, waiting around to do our sound check, and then a few more hours for the gig itself; endless hours hanging around in studios, waiting for the sound engineers to get the drum sound right, and then waiting while the other band members recorded their parts. (In the late 1980s, The Rolling Stones' drummer Charlie Watts was asked what it had been like, playing in the band for 25 years. 'Well it's been five years of working,' he said, 'and 20 years of hanging around.')

In theory, I could have used the empty time productively, and sometimes I did – for example, by reading, writing or meditating. But often I just felt too unsettled, tired or scatterbrained to focus my mind. Although other factors were involved, it's no coincidence that I suffered from depression during those four years, and was a heavy drinker for the only time in my life.

The problem for musicians is that their lives aren't active enough to keep their attention focused externally, and so it turns inward. They confront the psychological discord inside their minds, which creates feelings of boredom, discontent, anxiety, and even depression. They use drugs and drink as a way of escaping from these feelings.

Of course, pop stars aren't the only people to suffer from these problems. Many film stars have had problems with substance abuse too, and there are many cases of extremely rich people with similar difficulties. This seems to be a particular problem for people who are born into money. In the UK, there is a high incidence of drug problems among the aristocracy, for instance. There have been many cases of 'privileged' young aristocrats being arrested for heroin or cocaine possession, checking themselves into clinics for treatment, and/or dying due to drug problems.

One well-known example was the Marquis of Bristol, who died of multiple organ failure in 1999. He had a fortune of more than £30 million, which he used to try to keep his unhappiness at bay. He held lavish parties, owned a fleet of classic cars, a private helicopter, several houses and apartments around the world. But there was always a deep dissatisfaction inside him, and he eventually turned to drugs to try to escape it. His drug addiction killed him at the age of 44, but in reality, as one journalist wrote shortly after his death, he 'died of boredom.'

Another case was the tragic story of Constantine Niarchos, the son of the Greek shipping magnate Stavros Niarchos. Despite a fortune of £1 billion, Niarchos suffered from chronic depression and low self-esteem. In his mid-30s he took up mountaineering, and at first it seemed that the new sense of purpose and the self-discipline entailed by the sport was stabilizing him. But just two weeks after climbing Mount Everest, he committed suicide with a massive overdose of cocaine.

In view of this, it's not surprising that psychologists have found that extremely wealthy people are no happier than the rest of us. In the words of the psychologists Solomon, Greenberg, and Pyszcynski:

> *People with enormous amounts of money are, contrary to common folk wisdom, actually no happier than their less wealthy counterparts, and they are statistically more prone to depression and other forms of psychopathology[1].*

You might find this difficult to believe. How can these people be so unhappy when they have so much money and so much leisure time? After all, they're free of the niggling worries about paying bills and keeping up with the mortgage that oppress most of us. They can buy anything they want at any time, go anywhere in the world they want to, do anything they want to at any moment.

But again, the main factor here is too much empty time. To put it simply, people who don't need to work spend too much time alone with themselves, with nothing in particular to do. They aren't forced to fix their attention outside themselves for eight or nine hours a day, as most of us are. As a result they experience a great deal of inner discord and discontent.

This isn't just a problem for pop stars and aristocrats though. Many unemployed people face similar problems. Research shows that unemployed people are much more unhappy than the employed, with a higher level of suicide, alcoholism, drug addiction, and mental problems.[2] This isn't just because of a lack of activity and structure, of course – other factors include lower income, low social status and fewer social contacts – but it's certainly an important factor. Like my colleague Jimmy, retired people often suffer similar problems too. After a short 'honeymoon' period when they feel glad to be free of the pressure and the deadlines of work, they often begin start to feel disillusioned and even depressed.

A friend of my father was looking forward to retirement so much that he was counting down the days. He would phone my dad and say 'Only another 79 working days to go now! I can't wait!' He was an accounts manager at a factory and his job was stressful and demanding, so he was looking forward to spending his days pottering around the house, gardening and watching cricket in the summer. But when retirement came he found it dispiriting. After a few weeks, he began to complain about having too much time on his hands. He had a good pension so money wasn't a problem; not knowing what to do with himself was. Now he called my dad to say, 'Retirement's not all it's cracked up to be' or 'You might be fed up with your job now, but you'll miss it when it's gone.' Fortunately for him, after about six months another firm called and asked him to do some contract work.

It's strange to think that to a large extent the whole entertainment industry – TV, movies and DVDs, newspapers and magazines, computer games etc., – is fuelled by our inability to live inside ourselves. Modern culture offers us so many different – and massively effective – ways of keeping out attention focused outside ourselves that it's almost frightening. The seventeenth-century French mathematician and philosopher Pascal wrote that 'the sole cause of man's unhappiness is that he does not know how to stay quietly in his own room.' Pascal recognized a fundamental unhappiness in human beings that impelled them to constantly seek out diversions such as – in his day – warfare, dancing, hunting, and status-chasing. He recognized that 'this is why men are so fond of hustle and bustle; that is why prison is such a fearful punishment.'[3]

But in the twenty-first century, we don't need to go out into the world and hunt or make war. There's a massive array of diversions available to us *in* 'our rooms,' most of them via the Internet – social networking, e-mailing, texting, computer games and so on. (Even prison isn't as fearful as it was in Pascal's day, since modern prisoners have access to some distractions.) If you don't want to spend any time with your thoughts or your own being, all you have to do is keep your computer or your iPod turned on. In fact, the difficulty nowadays is *finding* some time to be alone with yourself.

Pascal wrote that to be a king was the most privileged state, because a king was surrounded by people 'whose only thought is to divert him and stop him thinking about himself.'[4] In this sense, we're practically all as privileged as kings.

It's also strange to think that a lot of the activity that fuels the world economy stems from our inability to do nothing. (Of course, this doesn't include the billions of people in less economically developed countries who have to work long hours just to survive.) If a large proportion of people gained the ability to *be* – and so lost the need for distraction – then the entertainment industry would suddenly become much smaller, and a lot of movie and sports stars would find themselves out of work, or with vastly reduced salaries. A huge amount of economic activity would suddenly stop too. Working hours would be reduced; people would only work as much as they needed and would stop using work simply as a way of keeping their attention focused outside themselves. As a result, the world economy would flounder. But this might not matter so much, since people who are able *to be* don't need to buy unnecessary material goods.

Of course, our need to keep busy is partly the result of social conditioning too. Our governments need to encourage us to keep doing in order to keep the world economy growing. The capitalist system treats time as a commodity, and we're taught that we should fill our hours with 'productive' activity. But it's more deep-rooted than this. Our impulse to be active is obviously a psychological need too.

This behavior may seem so normal and natural that you might wonder why I'm describing it as if it were a problem. But why should we spend almost all our time focusing our attention outside ourselves? Why should human beings feel this compulsion to be busy? Why do so many of us have to spend 28 hours a week staring at images on picture boxes in the corner of our rooms?

A lot of activity is necessary, of course, and extremely beneficial, both to others and ourselves. For example, the kind of 'active' absorption we experience when our minds are focused on creative and challenging tasks – such as writing a novel or creating a computer program, designing a new dress or playing chess – can be an extremely positive state. Activities such as these concentrate our mental energy, and make us feel more alert and alive. They quieten our normal thought-chatter and give us a sense of control over our minds. (Mihaly Csikszentmihalyi calls this state of absorption 'flow' and describes its positive effects in his book *Flow – The Psychology of Happiness*). These types of activities don't take us *out of* the present; they actually make us *more* present. They don't just let us escape from our psychological discord; they enable us to *heal* it. (We'll look at these activities in more detail later.)

Here I'm talking about activity that is neither necessary nor positive – activity we do just for its own sake and which can affect us negatively. Unfortunately 'flow' isn't such a common experience in our lives. Most of us spend more time in states of *passive* absorption, where there's no real challenge and we don't have to concentrate very hard. When we watch TV or surf the Internet we don't focus our mental energy, and so we don't experience a glow of wellbeing. In fact, the opposite is usually the case: after a few hours' watching TV you're more likely to feel drained of mental energy, with a sense of frustration and unease inside you.

The reason why inactivity causes these problems – why we often 'go to pieces' when we have too much time on our hands and spend too long alone with ourselves – is our psychological discord. The problem is that our own 'mind-space' – which we enter when our attention isn't focused externally – is a very uncomfortable place. Our 'psyche', the consciousness we feel ourselves to be inside our heads, is such an unpleasant place that it's difficult for us to spend any time there.

Think of two parents that argue all the time. There's a terrible atmosphere in their home. Every time their teenage daughter comes home she senses an atmosphere of hostility, which she knows can erupt into aggression at any moment. Every time she talks to her mother and father they're irritable and snap back at her. They're so wrapped up in their enmity for each other that they don't have any time for her. As a result, she tries to spend as much time as possible away from home, at her friends' houses or hanging around the park or local mall. She only goes back when it's absolutely necessary, for meals and for sleeping.

The atmosphere of hostility in the house is, of course, the psychological discord caused by humania. It pushes us out of ourselves, in the same way that the hostility pushes the girl out of her home.

CHAPTER 2
Psychological Discord

Humania has two main elements, which I'll describe in turn. Together, these two elements have many effects and consequences, which we'll also examine. The first element is 'ego-separateness' (or 'ego-isolation'); the second is 'cognitive discord.'

Ego-separateness/ego-isolation

When I was 18, in my first year at the University of Warwick, I had one of the most terrifying experiences of my life. A friend invited me to his room to smoke some marijuana. I'd tried dope – as we called it – once before in some cookies, and had a great time, feeling light-headed and relaxed and giggling like a child. I assumed I'd feel the same this time, but it couldn't have been more different. The dope must have been quite strong, because I started to feel strange after just a few drags. There were six or seven of us passing the joint around, and quite suddenly the atmosphere changed. There seemed to be some tension in the air. Nobody was speaking, and everyone seemed sullen. And suddenly it was clear: I was the reason for the bad atmosphere. The others didn't want me here. They all knew each other, they all had rooms on the same corridor, but I just knew Darren, who was on my course. Maybe it was because of my accent.

They were all southerners and I had strong northern English accent. It was obvious I didn't belong with them.

I wished I could have made a few friendly comments or jokes to ease the atmosphere, but it seemed impossible to talk. I felt trapped inside myself. The mechanism that turned my thoughts into speech had broken down, as if a connection had been cut. I sat there for what seemed like an eternity, feeling more and more unwelcome and uncomfortable, until finally I managed to stand up and say to Darren, 'I've got to get going.'

'Are you alright Steve?'

'Yeah, fine, I've just got to go.'

I left the halls of residence and walked through the students' union building, full of students drinking and talking and laughing, and felt a terrifying sense of isolation. I was completely alone here, trapped inside my own mental space with these thoughts, and this sense of being a conscious entity, and nobody would ever be able to really know me, to experience what I was experiencing, to feel what I was feeling. I felt incredibly lonely, like a planet surrounded by millions of miles of empty space, a terrible unbridgeable gulf between me and everyone else. The space inside my head where 'I' lived seemed cramped and oppressive, like a tiny dark prison cell.

I felt that I was experiencing the reality of my predicament as a human being, a terrible truth that everyone fought hard to avoid, and it seemed impossible to bear. It was the same for everyone else – we were all trapped inside ourselves, completely isolated and unknowable, and we were all trying so hard to escape, drinking and talking and watching TV to try to forget the emptiness inside us.

The effects of the dope faded away after a few hours, but this sense of isolation stayed with me – in a less acute form – for months afterward. Whenever I was with a group of people I had always had the sense that we were separate entities, trying to bridge the gulf between us by talking and making gestures, but never able to know each other, always alone within our own mental worlds, like islands trying to communicate with smoke signals across the sea.

You could see this experience as a drug-induced psychotic episode, but I think it was really only an amplification of an awareness that was already – and always, at least since my mid-teens – present within me. The drug gave me an acute insight into one of the essential realities of our normal human state, which all of us experience, even if we aren't conscious of it: the fact that we all exist in a state of 'ego-separateness' or 'ego-isolation.'

Separation

There are some peoples in the world – indigenous peoples like Aboriginal Australians or the tribal peoples of Polynesia – who don't seem to exist as individuals in the same way that we do. Their sense of individuality doesn't seem as sharp as ours. Their sense of identity *includes* nature and other people. Often they don't have fixed names; their names can change throughout their lives, and include those of other members of the tribe. Some indigenous peoples use tekonyms – terms that describe the relationship between two people – instead of personal or kinship names. For example, when a child is born, the mother's name might change to 'Mother-of...' and the father's to 'Father-of...'[1]

Similarly, many indigenous peoples see their identity as being bound up with their land. For example, according to the Fijian-born anthropologist A. Ravuvu, Fijians see their land as 'an extension of the concept of self. To most Fijians the idea of parting with one's *vanua* or land is tantamount to parting with one's life.'[2] This is why some indigenous peoples – such as the U'wa of Colombia or the Kaiowa of Brazil – have threatened to commit collective suicide if their land is taken from them. As the cultural psychologists Hazel Markus and Shinobu Kitayama put it, American–European peoples appear to function as 'independent selves,' whereas indigenous peoples have 'interdependent selves.'[3]

Most tribal peoples, at least those who still live a traditional way of life, are also very egalitarian. They have very few, if any, individual possessions. They don't own individual pieces of land, and share any food they collect. Many anthropologists have noted that indigenous groups don't even have words for concepts like 'possession' or 'property' or verbs meaning 'to own.'[4] It's as if, since they don't view themselves as separate entities, the concept of individual ownership has no meaning for them. If you don't separate your identity from other people, why would you need to separate your property and your food from theirs?

Children don't experience this sense of separateness either. They don't see themselves as separate from their experience; they don't have an 'I' that stands apart from what they're doing and analyzes their experience. This is one of the reasons why childhood is so wonderful. Children feel connected to everything around them, in a participatory flow with all experience, with no 'in here' or 'out there.' The sense of separateness develops slowly as we move into adolescence, becoming firmly established in our late teens. The ego develops as a structure, creating a sense of 'inner-ness' and 'walling us off.'

However, we have a stronger sense of individuality than these traditional indigenous peoples or than children. The boundaries of our egos are stronger and more defined, creating a sense of duality between the world and us. We're 'in here,' trapped inside our heads, while the rest of the cosmos and all other human beings are 'out there.' As a result, our egalitarian impulses are weaker, and we have a stronger need to accumulate wealth and possessions *for ourselves.*

This strong sense of individuality creates some major psychological problems for us. On the one hand, it creates a basic sense of *aloneness.* Whereas traditional indigenous peoples feel a sense of connection to the world, we feel *dis*connected from it. We're always observing rather than participating, looking out *at* the world, rather than being a part *of* it. We can communicate with other people by speaking, writing or gesturing, but they will never be able to truly know us, or to share our thoughts and feelings. Our inner being will always be sealed off from them.

This 'ego-isolation' also creates a sense of *incompleteness.* We're separate from the world and, like fragments that have broken off from the whole, feel a sense of insufficiency. There's a kind of hole inside us that we spend most of our lives trying to fill (but very rarely succeed), like kittens taken away from their mother at birth and always hankering for affection and attention, to compensate for a sense of lack.

Born-again Christians mean something close to this when they say that there is a 'God-shaped hole' inside us –

although in my view, religion can't fill the hole either, only provide the same (ultimately incomplete) consolation as wealth or success. This is why, as Chief Mountain Lake remarked, we always seem to be seeking something. We're seeking something to try to complete ourselves.

As a result of this aloneness and incompleteness, we don't feel completely 'at home' in the world. We feel somehow adrift, as if we don't fully belong, like people who have traveled the world so often that they no longer feel rooted anywhere. Whereas traditional indigenous peoples seem to perceive the world as a benign and benevolent place, to us it seems indifferent and even vaguely malevolent.

Fear of death

Another psychological problem caused by ego-separateness is an acute fear of death. We live our whole lives from the standpoint of the separate self, in service of the ego. We spend our time trying to satisfy the ego's desires or to compensate for our sense of isolation and the lack it creates. We form beliefs, make relationships, build careers, chase after hopes and ambitions – all on its behalf. And so the idea that this omnipotent ego-self will one day cease to exist understandably terrifies us. Since indigenous people share their sense of identity with their tribe and their land, their individual death doesn't have such massive significance. A part of their being will live on through the land and their tribe. But since our sense of identity is wholly bound up with our ego, when we die, *everything* dies – all of the future and the past, all of our achievements and ambitions, our possessions and status, vanishing like a vast palace suddenly razed to the ground by an earthquake.

Even if we might not be conscious of it, this fear of death is always at the back of our minds, creating an undercurrent of anxiety and exacerbating the sense of insecurity and insignificance created by our fragile egos. Some people deal with this anxiety by convincing themselves that when they die their egos will live on forever in an idyllic new world, free from all of the suffering that filled their lives on earth. Others simply try to forget about it, to avoid thinking or talking about it, and pretend it's not going to happen. In largely non-religious countries like the UK, death has become a taboo subject, a five-letter word. If anyone broaches the subject there's usually a long hushed pause, and an abrupt shift to a different topic.

In this way, our ego-separateness creates psychological discord. It makes our mental space an uncomfortable place to be. When we're alone, without any distractions or activities on which to latch our attention, we *feel* our essential aloneness and incompleteness, and experience the undercurrent of anxiety in our minds, even though we might not actually be aware of them as the source of our discomfort.

'Thought-chatter'

As an experiment now, stop reading this book and close your eyes. After a few seconds you'll probably become aware of the thoughts buzzing away inside your mind. Let these thoughts go wherever they want, just observe them, as they keep streaming through...

Let them stream through your mind for about two minutes, then think back to the first thought that you were aware of, and retrace the steps from there to your final thought.

You'll most likely be amazed at the number of different thoughts you've had, and the strange twists and turns they've taken. They could have leapt from one side of the world to another, from 20 years in the past to a few years in the future, from a book you read a few months ago to a poem you read last week, to a song you heard on the radio this morning to a person you went to school with to a celebrity you read about in a newspaper story...

Sometimes when you're listening to a CD – perhaps in the car – you might tell yourself 'I love that part of the song; I'd like to listen to it again.' You return to the appropriate place on the CD, and then, perhaps 20 to 30 seconds later, you realize that the section has already passed by, and you've missed it. It was on, but you weren't paying attention and didn't *hear it.* And so you have to go back again. And usually – although not always – the second time you manage to hold your attention on the music.

This might also happen when you find yourself looking forward to eating some food – perhaps your favorite takeout or a bar of chocolate. A few mouthfuls into the meal, or a few bites into the chocolate, you might realize that you've missed it. You've been eating, but haven't actually *tasted it.*

The problem in these situations is that your attention is taken away from the music and the food by the 'thought-chatter' inside your head – the stream of memories, worries, and imaginations of future situations. Within a second or two of rewinding the CD – or starting the meal – these random associations start to flow through your mind and absorb your attention, leaving little or none for the sensory experiences of sound or taste.

A similar thing can happen when you're driving. You might suddenly realize that you're at a particular point in your daily journey to work and can't remember the last minute or two. You changed lanes, turned off, stopped at the traffic lights and turned left, all without realizing what you were doing. This can be a little frightening. How did you manage to drive without being aware of what you were doing, while being unconscious? What if someone had run out into the road, or a car had suddenly pulled in front of you? Luckily you're so used to driving – and your particular route – that you can do it completely automatically, like eating while reading the newspaper.

What has happened here is that your attention has been completely absorbed in thought-chatter. You have been completely 'elsewhere.' Driving is automatic to you now, so you don't need to pay conscious attention to it, and so you're able to give all of your attention to your daydreams and memories.

'Thought-chatter' has a powerful momentum. Once it starts it's almost impossible to stop it. When I was younger I sometimes felt as if it was driving me mad. I'd lie in bed for hours at night, unable to sleep because of the thoughts racing through my mind, replaying some of the day's conversations or situations, songs I'd heard or creating imaginary scenarios for the future. I felt as if my mind had been overtaken by a crazed chatterbox, and wanted to shout 'shut up and let me go to sleep!'

Occasionally when I went for walks I'd look at the countryside or up at the sky, and would *know* that they were beautiful, but be unable to perceive the beauty, again, because of the chaotic thoughts buzzing through my mind. (As the poet Samuel Coleridge complained, while staring at the moon and stars, 'I see them all so excellently fair/ I see, not *feel,* how beautiful they are.' [5]) Fortunately my thought-chatter has since slowed down and I have more control over it now.

Anyone who has ever meditated will be aware of the sheer power of thought-chatter. In meditation we usually use a focusing device – a mantra (a sound, which is repeated silently in the mind), a candle flame, your breath or other methods – to try to quiet our minds and develop a degree of inner stillness. But sometimes it just doesn't work. Thought-chatter is so powerful that it keeps taking your attention away from the mantra, and you have to keep bringing yourself out of your thoughts and refocusing on it. Usually your mind does become quiet if you persevere, but sometimes it's so wild that you simply have to give up. Beginners in meditation sometimes find it unnerving to come face-to-face with the sheer wildness and force of their thought-chatter. It may disturb them so much that after a couple of sessions they may decide that meditation isn't for them after all. But it's important to remember that with regular meditation – even though it may be difficult in the beginning – your mind does gradually become quieter.

The 'default setting' of the mind

Usually we call this mental activity 'thinking', but this isn't really accurate. 'Thinking' suggests something active, over which we have conscious control, but almost all of our 'thinking' isn't like this. It's almost always random and involuntary. It runs through our heads whether we like it or not. That's why I prefer the term 'thought-chatter,' or 'cognitive discord.' Whenever our attention isn't occupied externally, thought-chatter is always there, like a machine that's always on standby, ready to start up the moment our mind releases itself from any external 'attention hook.' It's what you could call our mind's 'default setting.'

Real thinking is when we consciously use powers of reason and logic to evaluate different options, deliberate over problems, decisions and plans, and so forth. We often like to think of ourselves as 'rational' creatures, superior to animals because we can 'reason,' but this kind of rational thinking is actually quite rare. (Even when it comes to decisions and plans, a lot of the choices we make and the strategies we use are instinctive rather than the result of deliberation.) And in fact, thought-chatter makes it harder to use our rational powers because, when we do have issues to deliberate, it streams through our minds and diverts our attention. For example, imagine you're trying to decide what to buy your husband or wife for an anniversary present. While you're thinking about it memories of your wedding day run through your mind and then of your honeymoon in Italy which reminds you about a scandal you recently read about the Italian prime minister which sets you thinking about the political situation in this country which reminds you that have to file your taxes... It's so difficult to focus your thoughts that no ideas come into your mind, and you have to ask your colleagues at work what they would like as a gift if it were their anniversary.

Being immersed in thought-chatter isn't so different from dreaming – at least, the kind of associative dreaming that sorts through the impressions and information we've absorbed recently and sends a strange mixture of them back through our minds. (There may well be other, more meaningful, types of dreaming from deeper levels of the mind, which hold symbolic significance and connect with what Jung called the 'collective unconscious.') We have a little more control over thought-chatter than dreams, and it comes from the conscious mind rather than the subconscious, but essentially it's the same whirl of mental material. (Of course, this is suggested by the term 'daydreaming.') And, as we'll see later, stopping thought-chatter *is* like waking up out of a dream, bringing a new, clear awareness and a new relationship to reality. Thought-chatter is similar to daydreaming, although rather than being one and the same, I think daydreaming is best seen as a *type* of thought-chatter – an intense state of absorption in imaginary mental scenarios, usually in a more relaxed state of mind.

There are two situations when we experience thought-chatter. One is when an activity isn't interesting or challenging enough to hold our attention. When we do household chores and other automatic tasks, they aren't demanding or interesting enough to hold our attention, and so our attention turns inside, to the thoughts and day-dreams running inside our heads. This could happen at work too, if your job isn't particularly challenging or interesting. If you're stacking shelves, pouring cups of tea or packing clothes, you only need to give a small degree of attention to these tasks, and so at the same time you're partly immersed in thoughts about what you're going to do at the weekend or reminiscences of your last trip away.

The second situation is between activities, when there's nothing external there to fix our attention to. You could be waiting for a train, or for the kettle to boil, in the bathroom or lying in bed in the morning or at night – in these situations your mind normally fills with thought-chatter too.

This thought-chatter is such a normal part of our experience that, again, many of us take it completely for granted. But from an objective standpoint, it's actually quite bizarre. Why should we have a voice in our heads all the time, a noise and image-producing machine constantly recalling our experience, replaying bits of information we've absorbed, and imagining scenarios before they've occurred? Why should our minds jump so chaotically and randomly from one association to the next? People with schizophrenia are considered to be insane because they hear voices in their heads – but is our 'normal' thought-chatter really so different? It should really be seen as a kind of madness as well – or at least as a kind of design fault, a malfunctioning of the human mind.

Cognitive discord

Short periods of thought-chatter can sometimes seem pleasurable, particularly the daydreaming type. It's pleasant to lie down on a beach or on the sofa, and create mental scenarios of you satisfying your desires and ambitions, or to relive pleasant past events or 'look forward' to future ones.

But with most thought-chatter, it's usually not long before you start to feel a little uncomfortable, and feel an impulse to escape it by immersing your attention in something external. This was illustrated by a 2010 study at Harvard University in which researchers used an iPhone app to track people's moods and thoughts at different times. The researchers, Matthew Killingsworth and Dan Gilbert, contacted 2,250 volunteers at random times, asking them how happy they were, what they were doing, and what they were thinking about. The study found that the volunteers spent around half their time with a 'wandering mind,' thinking about things other than what they were doing. The study highlighted the negative effects of thought-chatter: people who spent more time with a wandering mind were found to be more prone to depression, and found it more difficult to relax. As Killingsworth and Gilbert concluded:

> *This study shows that our mental lives are pervaded, to a remarkable degree, by the nonpresent. A human mind is a wandering mind, and a wandering mind is an unhappy mind... The ability to think about what is not happening is a cognitive achievement that comes at an emotional cost[6].*

Part of the reason for this is simply that thought-chatter creates a constant *disturbance* inside us. In the words of the German mystic Meister Eckhart, we experience 'a storm of inward thought[7].' Our mind is filled with chaos of swirling thoughts that we have little or no control over, and so we feel unsettled and uneasy, just as we do when there is a loud disturbance *outside* us. It creates what Csikszentmihalyi calls 'psychic entropy' – a lack of control over our own minds. It's discordant because it's random and (almost) uncontrollable.

Also, as the examples above show, thought-chatter creates a barrier between us and our experience. It stops us experiencing the world in an immediate way. It creates a fog of abstraction in our minds, which dilutes and obscures all our experience, everything we see, hear, smell, feel or touch, so that reality becomes a shadow. It may even create a sense of unreality, when the memories, images, and scenarios in our minds appear more real than our actual experience.

Perhaps the biggest problem with thought-chatter, however, is that it's often tinged with negativity. Thoughts about the future are tinged with worry and anxiety, thoughts about the past are tinged with regret or bitterness, and thoughts about your present life situation are tinged with dissatisfaction.

This has a major impact on our lives because negative thoughts create negative states of mind. If a friend or colleague makes a negative comment to you, it makes you feel angry or depressed, and we react in exactly the same way to negative thought-chatter. Some negative thoughts may be so habitual and firmly fixed that they form a 'script' of worrying and self-critical thoughts running constantly through our minds. Your 'script' might keep repeating, *'I don't deserve this – I'm not meant to be happy;' 'I can't do this – I know it's going to go wrong;'* or *'She's much more attractive/successful/happy than me – why can't I be like her?'* These scripts create feelings of anxiety and discontent, and create a lack of self-confidence and poor self-image.

This is why cognitive therapies, such as Cognitive Behavioral Therapy (CBT), can be effective. The premise of CBT is that our thoughts determine our moods and feelings. The aim of the therapy is to identify habitual negative thoughts, and then try to replace them with more objective or positive thoughts. In other words, it aims to 'reprogram' the underlying 'scripts' of our thought-chatter. And in the short term at least, this can have very positive effects. Research has shown, for example, that CBT is as effective as medication in treating depression and anxiety, and can even alleviate the physical symptoms of diseases such as cancer and rheumatoid arthritis[8].

But why are our thoughts so negative, you might ask? Why do we usually focus on the negative rather than the positive? Why do we interpret the future pessimistically rather than optimistically, dwell on what we're dissatisfied with in the present rather than what we should be grateful for, and mull over negative events from the past rather than the good things that have happened to us?

The reason for this, I believe, is simply that the atmosphere of our psyche is already charged with negativity because of our ego-isolation. There's an atmosphere of slight unease and anxiety that tinges our thoughts with negativity.

The pliability of our minds is part of the problem too. Particularly during childhood, the human psyche is amazingly plastic and pliable. This is why beliefs passed on by our parents can be so difficult to question or dislodge. Absorbed during childhood, the most bizarre beliefs can become part of the deep structure of our psyche, and so stay with us for the rest of our lives, so deep-rooted that we take them completely for granted. This is often how religious beliefs are passed on. Hence the old Jesuit saying, 'Give me the child till the age of seven and I will show you the man.'

This is also true of trauma. If we experience any form of abuse or neglect – again, particularly during childhood – then the psyche may carry that damage for the rest of our lives (unless we have appropriate psychotherapy). And a similar process occurs with negative thought-patterns. If our parents pass on negative thought-patterns to us – either through their verbalized negative attitudes, or by treating us as if we're worthless or unlovable - then these negative thoughts may solidify into 'scripts' or 'schemata.' These become what might be called 'cognitive habits' that determine the attitude and tone of our thoughts, and cause a lack of self-worth and confidence.

This doesn't just happen during childhood though. Even during adulthood 'cognitive habits' can form quickly, and become fixed into our minds. Once a negative experience is repeated a number of times, it can easily harden into a neurosis or phobia. A person who has two or three rough crossings on a ferry may develop a long-term phobia about sailing. A person who is left by two different lovers may develop a permanent insecurity and fear of being abandoned. A person who spends a few months living next door to noisy neighbors may develop a lifelong over-sensitivity to noise.

The positive side of this, however, is that, since the mind is so plastic, it can also be remolded in a *positive* way. Cognitive habits can be changed fairly easily – in fact; this is the whole purpose of CBT. Even deep structural trauma dating from childhood can be healed through psychotherapy.[8]

Thought-chatter wouldn't be such a big problem if we didn't *identify* with it. When we stand back from our thoughts and just watch them flow by, we aren't so affected by them. (We often do this when daydreaming, which is another way that daydreaming is different from normal thought-chatter.) We're able to say to ourselves: *Oh well, there goes another negative thought – I don't have to pay attention to it.* But most of the time our identity is bound up with our thoughts. We can't separate ourselves from them. We believe that we *are* this crazy random thought-generator, with its negative scripts – and so we're powerless against them, and allow them to determine our moods and sense of self-worth.

Again, I'm not arguing that thought-chatter is *completely* negative. Besides giving us the occasional pleasure of sitting back and watching our minds wandering to and fro, some psychologists have suggested that daydreaming may have a purpose as a kind of 'social rehearsal,' allowing us to prepare for situations and events. The daydreaming state can also be a kind of 'cauldron of creativity,' which gives rise to insights and ideas. For example, Einstein daydreamed the Theory of Relativity while working as a clerk in a patents office. Composers such as Brahms and Debussy purposely used the daydreaming state as an aid to composing. As the American philosopher John Dewey remarked, creative insights often occur when people are 'relaxed to the point of reverie.'[9]

Unfortunately though, most thought-chatter is much more negative than the daydreaming type. The problem with thought-chatter generally is that it's *too* uncontrollable, *too* negative, and that we identify with it too much.

Too close to reality

When I was about 14 years old, a neighbor had a nervous breakdown. He had a drinking problem, had never married and was known as something of a loner. Always very bright, he had been expected to become an academic, perhaps a university professor, but had ended up as a schoolteacher instead, living with his mother in his childhood home. One morning, he decided he couldn't face the world and locked himself in his room. His mother had to phone the police, and he only opened the door after they threatened to break it down. After that he never went to back to his job, and hardly ever left his house. We would only occasionally see him walking to the shops to buy bottles of whiskey, looking unkempt and anxious.

His breakdown was probably the result of his isolation, his frustration and his alcoholism, but at the time several people made comments like 'he's too intelligent for his own good' or 'he thinks too much.' The implication was that by thinking so much and being intelligent he had somehow come too close to reality, and glimpsed terrible truths human beings aren't supposed to see. As a result, he couldn't face the world or live a normal life anymore.

In our culture, there is a widespread taboo against 'thinking.' It's seen as dangerous to be 'deep,' to start analyzing your situation and questioning the values you live by. In popular folklore, the more intelligent and introspective you are, the more vulnerable you are to depression or even suicide. This is closely linked to fear of death – there is a belief that if we start contemplating the fact that we're going to die one day and could die at any moment, it's bound to make us depressed and wonder what the point of doing anything is. This gives people some justification for filling their free time with activities and distractions: to avoid thinking about their predicament.

And it's true that, from the standpoint of our normal state of being, reality does seem bleak. Through the prism of humania, the world appears an indifferent and inanimate place, and our lives may seem meaningless. It may seem that we're just born into this world by accident, and wander about its surface for a few decades, struggling to satisfy our needs as our bodies slowly decay, until they're so decrepit that they can't function anymore. Then we vanish with hardly a trace, almost as if we never existed in the first place. (Of course, I don't believe that this *is* the reality of our predicament, but a false picture created by our disordered psyche. In my view, as I'll explain later, the reality of our predicament is much more benevolent.)

But at the same time very few people actually contemplate these 'truths' when their minds are unoccupied. Most people's minds are much more microcosmic. People who 'think too much' don't have problems because of the terrible truths they discover about life, but because thinking exposes them to too much psychological discord. We don't need distraction so much to avoid contemplating our reality (as Pascal believed), but to avoid experiencing our inner discord. It isn't reality that is the problem, so much as our minds. The monster isn't out there; it's inside us.

The flight from discord

And so who can blame us for wanting to escape from the effects of ego-madness, from the swirling chaos of our thoughts, and the negative feelings they produce? Spending time with our minds is like being in the company of a mad miserable person who drives you crazy, never stopping talking or sitting down, telling you about his or her problems and complaining about the world.

Not only that, our ego-isolation means that we're completely on our own with this person, in the middle of nowhere, hundreds of miles away from the nearest town, with no means of communicating with anyone.

In the same way that we don't enjoy being on a noisy and crowded city street, and rush home as quickly as possible to get away from it, we hate to be stuck in the noisy, cramped and negative space of our psyche. We're impelled to escape from the discord, and – as many pop stars, young aristocrats and unemployed and retired people have found – we're liable to suffer from chronic dissatisfaction and depression when we spend too much time there.

Our normal state is one of disturbance, negativity, isolation, and incompleteness. The *structure* of the psyche (i.e. its strong ego-boundary) creates isolation, incompleteness and anxiety. The *activity* of the psyche (i.e. its constant thought-chatter) produces disturbance and negativity. And together this constitutes humania.

It's important to remember that there's nothing natural or inevitable about this state. It's not just 'the way things are,' or part of the 'human condition.' In the same way that the bleak vision of reality generated by humania is not objective, the state of ego-separation and cognitive discord we experience is only a *particular* state of being, rather than an absolute one. This is shown by the fact that, as we've seen, there are many other peoples in the world who appear to exist in a different state of being, without apparently suffering from humania – and also by the fact that, as we'll see later, most of us frequently experience a different state of being, and some of us even manage to shift into a different state permanently.

A large part of everything we experience and everything we do – the moods and mental states we experience, how we live our lives on a day-to-day basis, our values, and goals – is determined by humania. In fact, it could be said that the desire to avoid facing psychological discord – or to compensate for it – is the main motivating force of many people's lives. In the same way that a person who is seriously ill may spend most of their time trying to cope with their illness, we spend much of our time trying to deal with this mental disorder.

In the next few chapters, we're going to examine the different ways that we do this, looking at some of the ways in which humania manifests in our lives.

CHAPTER 3

The Subtle Effects of Humania

The effects of humania can be subtle. You might occasionally catch yourself feeling a mild sense of unease, the kind you usually feel when you're worried about a small problem. You stop to wonder what it is you're worried about and are surprised to find that there doesn't seem to be anything there. There's nothing in the future that you feel anxious about and nothing in the past that you feel angry or embarrassed about. This uneasiness doesn't seem to have any tangible source. So why do you feel worried when there's nothing to worry about?

You might be in a situation where you have every reason to be happy – a relaxing evening at home, sitting on your lawn on a summer's day, or even in a luxurious hotel room – but there's a sense that 'something's not quite right.' You have the sense that there's something you need to do, even though you've no idea what; you have a feeling that something's going to go wrong, or that there's something missing. It's difficult to pin it down exactly, as if there's some kind of 'psychological worm' crawling through your mind-space, but you can't sense it clearly enough to define.

In this situation you're simply experiencing the undercurrent of unease that's always in our minds, but is so familiar that we often don't recognize its presence. This undercurrent has tangible effects when it tinges our thoughts with worry and bitterness, but here you're experiencing it in its pure form, as an atmosphere of negativity that pervades our mental space.

The sense of unease is closely related to a sense of dissatisfaction. Because we feel that something isn't right, we feel a desire to *make* things right. We feel a constant desire to change things, to add things to ourselves, to improve our situation. But we make the 'causal error' of assuming that the cause of our dissatisfaction is outside us rather than inside. We assume that the way to find satisfaction is by changing our life situations rather than ourselves. We redecorate our houses, treat ourselves to a new kitchen, a new carpet or a new car, and change our hairstyles and clothes. All of these might give us a short-lived sense of wellbeing, but dissatisfaction is still inside us, untouched by these external changes, and soon it rises to the surface again.

Loneliness and boredom

Some of our more obvious psychological problems are also the direct experience of our psychological discord. What we call 'loneliness' is often the direct experience of our ego-isolation, with a yearning to communicate with other people to try to alleviate it. When we're lonely we *feel* our fundamental isolation and incompleteness. Of course, human beings are social animals; it's not natural for us to be completely solitary. But our dislike of solitude is exaggerated by ego-madness. Humania impels us to avoid solitude as much as possible.

It's worth remembering that solitude and loneliness are two different things. In the right frame of mind – in a state of inner harmony – it's easy to be alone, even for long periods, without feeling lonely. In his poem *The Uprooted,* D.H. Lawrence vividly portrays the connection between ego-isolation and loneliness. As he writes, 'People who complain of loneliness must have lost something,/Lost some living connection with the cosmos, out of themselves... like a plant whose roots are cut.' For Lawrence himself, who lived in an intense state of connection with the world around him, 'To be alone is one of life's greatest delights... feeling oneself uninterrupted in the rooted connection with the centre of all things.'[1]

Boredom is the state of mental discomfort we feel when our attention isn't fixed to an external object. The discomfort we feel is the discord of our minds – the disturbance of our thought-chatter leaping to and fro, and the fundamental anxiety of our ego-isolation. When we say, 'I'm bored – I need something to do', what we're really saying is 'I'm feeling some psychological discord, and I need an activity or distraction to take me out of myself.'

Television and psychological discord

In terms of its effects on our lives, the main way that humania affects us is by generating the need for distraction and activity, as described in Chapter 1. And from the point of view of an alien anthropologist, perhaps the strangest of all these methods of distraction would be watching television. You can imagine the alien walking down a typical suburban street one evening, looking through people's windows and seeing TV sets flickering in room after room, with family after family sitting immobile, staring blankly at the images. 'What's happened to these people?' it might ask itself. 'Who has put them all into a trance?'

I said earlier that TV is the best method yet devised of keeping our attention focused outside ourselves, which is the same as saying that it's the best method yet devised of escaping our psychological discord. And because it's the best method, it's also the most popular (although it's become a little less popular since the growth of Internet-based entertainments and game consoles.)

TV is so hypnotically absorbing, and demands so little mental effort, that it enables us to escape from our own mental space for hours at a time. Books can have the same effect, but they demand more concentration, and so it's easier for our attention to become 'unlatched' from them. With television, all you have to do is press the 'on' button and within a few seconds you've escaped from psychological discord.

At other times, if we're not watching television in a focused way, it can serve as a kind of attention 'safety net,' while we're busy with other activities. (Radio often serves this function too.) The background noise of TV or radio gives us a sense of security, since it fills any potentially painful moments of silence and inattention, when we might have to touch into our psychological discord. Unfortunately many people have grown so used to this background chatter that they can't bear to be in their homes without it. When they open their front doors and walk into their living rooms, the silence feels unsettling and even slightly threatening, and so almost the first thing they do is fill it with media chatter.

People are sometimes surprised by my hostility toward television. For a long time I was a militant anti-televisionist. I didn't have a TV for over ten years. I had an ongoing battle with the TV licensing company – they didn't believe that I didn't have one, and kept demanding payment of my license fee. Especially in the early 1990s, before the Internet, mobile phones, and even computers, people were amazed that I could live without a TV. In one of my office jobs, a colleague once asked me if I'd seen last night's episode of a popular soap opera. 'No, I haven't got a television set,' I replied. The lady was amazed. 'So what do you *do*?' she asked in bemusement.

I've mellowed a little since then. We do have a television now, although one so small that we can't watch any foreign films, because the subtitles are too small to read. Now I probably watch TV for an average of half an hour a day – I like to keep up with the news, and sometimes we watch comedy programs or films.

One of the reasons why I don't like television is simply because I think it has a detrimental psychological effect. It's such an easy, passive form of entertainment that it weakens our powers of concentration. I was brought up as a TV addict – the television was always on in our house, and I probably watched it for an average of four or five hours a day, until I left home when I was 18. As a consequence, I had very poor powers of concentration. When I was about 17, I started to get interested in books, but found it very difficult to concentrate for more than a couple of pages at a time. I had to use all my willpower to resist the impulse to turn on the TV and keep my eyes focused on the text. It was the same when I started writing, a couple of years later – it was a struggle to keep my mind focused for more than a few minutes.

In fact, that was one of the reasons why I decided to stop watching television, so that I could strengthen my powers of concentration. I was aware that concentration is like a muscle, which has to be built up slowly, so I would force myself to sit still and write for slightly longer periods every week. Once I had managed to sit down and write for an hour, I increased the time to an hour and 15 minutes, and so on. And eventually, after a year or so, it became easy. The 'muscle' of my concentration was so strong that I could sit at my desk and write for hours at a time. Knowing what we do now about neuroplasticity, I would say this was a process of strengthening the area of my brain connected to attention (probably in my prefrontal cortex), making connections between the cells there and generating new cells, until there was so much 'gray matter' in the area that it was easy for me to concentrate for long periods.

Another problem with TV – and the media in general – is that it provides an alternate reality that makes us less interested in the real world. It makes us less interested in our own lives, and less interested in making changes in them. If you eavesdrop a conversation in a shop, an office or a café, there's a good chance that, rather than talking about their own lives, people will be chatting about TV shows or media celebrities. And it's not so imperative to make our own lives more fulfilling or exciting when there's so much stimulation and excitement to be found in this unreal parallel world.

But most of all, I dislike television because its primary function is to put us into a mental slumber, to blot out reality: to take us out of ourselves, out of our environment, and out of the present, so that we don't have to face our psychological discord.

Other drugs and addiction

Because of this mind-numbing and reality-removing effect, some psychologists have suggested that television should be seen as a drug. And whether or not this is the case, there's no doubt that another effect of humania is to predispose us to taking *actual* drugs, including alcohol. Pop stars and aristocrats may be a lot more vulnerable to drug and drink problems than the rest of us, but most of us are susceptible to them to some degree.

The urge to take drugs seems to be natural for human beings and, so far as we can tell, we've always taken them. There is evidence of drug-taking going back several thousand years – betel leaves were being chewed as a drug in southeast Asia 9,000 years ago, and a 1,000 years later, opium was being used as a drug in the Mediterranean[2].

The human impulse to take drugs can take two forms, which might be called 'transcendent' and 'escapist.' Sometimes drugs are taken as a way of intensifying consciousness and gaining access to levels of reality normally hidden from us. Psychedelic drugs – such as LSD or magic mushrooms – are often used for this 'transcendent' purpose. And this is particularly true of the drugs taken by indigenous peoples, usually as a part of initiation ceremonies, religious rites or to aid shamanic journeys.

But for us at least, drugs are mainly used for 'escapist' reasons, to allow us some respite from our psychological discord. People sometimes say that they 'want to get out of it' by getting drunk or taking drugs, and what they want to get out *of* is their ego-madness, their cognitive discord, and the isolation and incompleteness of the separate self.

Like TV, some drugs can create a state of suspended animation, numbing us to our discord. This is true of drugs such as alcohol, heroin and other depressants and tranquillizers. They can completely wipe away the negativity inside our minds, remove our compulsion to be active and take away the frustration we feel when we have too much unstructured time. On the other hand, some drugs – stimulants like cocaine or ecstasy – don't numb to our discontent so much as *override* it with pleasurable sensations. They make us feel so good that we just don't feel our psychological discord anymore.

The problem is that drugs always wear off. Our discord and discontent are always waiting in the wings, ready to re-emerge. And in the long run, drugs make our normal psychological state even more chaotic and unhealthy, and lead to the horrors of physical dependency.

Different degrees of humania

These are some of the visible signs and symptoms of humania. If you suffer from boredom, loneliness, need distractions such as TV and drink or take drugs – that is, if you're a normal human being – then you can clearly be diagnosed with the condition.

But every illness and disorder affects people differently, and the same is true of humania. Although almost all of us have the condition, we don't all suffer to the same degree.

Some people have such a high level of psychological discord inside them that – like the teacher friend of mine above – they can't be inactive for a minute, and can't spend any time alone. They have a very low boredom and loneliness threshold, and probably a stronger-than-usual need to 'get out of it' with alcohol or drugs. This might be due to a stronger-than-usual sense of ego-isolation. The boundaries of their ego may happen to be stronger and thicker, so that they feel more separate and more incomplete. Or it might be due to a higher-than-usual cognitive discord. Their thought-chatter may be so incessant that they can never turn off their mind. They might manage to sleep after a couple of drinks or sleeping tablets, but if they wake up in the middle of the night, the chatter immediately starts up again and keeps them awake until dawn.

Another person's thought-chatter may be more negative than normal. They may have absorbed a lot of negative scripts from their parents, and so constantly think self-critical thoughts. Because of this, any short period of introspection – just a few seconds of thought-chatter at a bus stop or between TV shows – may be enough to make them feel depressed.

Psychological discord can also be intensified by trauma. Trauma can cause 'structural damage' to the psyche. If parents abuse or neglect a young child – as the child's psyche is forming, and is very pliable – his or her ego will become even more fragile and separate than normal, with an acute sense of incompleteness and insecurity. Traumatic experiences also leave a residual pain within the psyche; a permanent psychological wound causing pain every time a person turns their attention inward. As a result, people who have suffered trauma may find it even more difficult to be alone with themselves, or to be inactive.

As well as trauma, our 'base level' psychological discord can be intensified – or emphasized – by other mental disorders. *The Diagnostic and Statistical Manual of Mental Disorders* lists more than 300 types of mental disorders, the main categories being clinical disorders – e.g. schizophrenia, depression, and anxiety disorders – and personality disorders – e.g. paranoia, narcissistic personality disorder and obsessive–compulsive disorder (OCD).

Many of these disorders have much more serious effects than our base level psychological discord, causing a great deal more psychological suffering. However, some milder disorders can actually be seen as manifestations of the condition. For example, anxiety disorders may be caused by cognitive discord, when negative thought-chatter creates a sense of dread of the future and a sense of guilt and bitterness about the past.

Ego-madness can be a cause of depression too. Depression is sometimes just simply the result of spending too much time inside our minds, experiencing too much inner discord. It's often the result of too much exposure to the disturbance of our thoughts and listening to their negativity – replaying the negative scripts we've picked up from our parents, anticipating unwelcome future events or recalling negative experiences from the past – together with too much exposure to the isolation and incompleteness of our minds. The best evidence for this is that, as we've seen, there appears to be a strong correlation between the amount of unstructured time that people have and how prone they are to depression and other psychological disorders.

In general, the more psychological discord a person experiences – either because they just happen to be born with a higher level of cognitive discord and ego-separateness, or because their basic discord is exacerbated by trauma or other mental disorders – the more vulnerable they are to substance abuse, or to drug addiction. Many scientific studies have shown, for example, that trauma in early life – such as sexual, physical or emotional abuse – increases a person's vulnerability to drug addiction.[3] Other research has shown that when traumatic events occur during adulthood, people often start to use drugs or alcohol as a coping mechanism, between six to 18 months afterward. Recovering alcoholics start drinking again, people who were abstinent start drinking, and current drinkers start drinking more.[4] When psychological discord reaches a high level, distractions like TV or work aren't enough. Being drunk or stoned may be the only way of gaining respite from the bombardment or negativity of our thought-chatter, our sense of incompleteness or from residual psychic pain.

In contrast, there are some people who aren't as affected by humania, and have a lower level of discord in their minds. People like this are happy in their own company and live a slow and relatively quiet life, not needing to fill their days with constant activity or distraction. They may not seem to 'do' very much but never complain about being bored or even about being lonely. They don't have a strong need to get drunk or stoned. They may prefer reading books to watching TV, and get enjoyment from relatively sedate activities such as cooking, walking in the countryside, or gardening. They don't need to live outside themselves all the time.

This is possible because their 'mental space' is more harmonious and comfortable than normal. Perhaps their 'ego-isolation' is less acute than normal, and they experience less cognitive discord, with quieter minds and a more positive bias to their thoughts. This could just be an accident of birth, or perhaps it's partly because of their lifestyle, a consequence of living a sedate life in a quiet area, regularly doing yoga or meditation, or going swimming or long-distance running. Or perhaps they have managed to heal their humania to a degree – as we will discuss later.

There are also a very small minority of people – like children and some indigenous peoples – who appear to be *completely* free of the condition, and live in a state of permanent and constant harmony. These are sometimes called 'enlightened' or 'self-actualized' people. The 'shifters' I described in my last book *Out of the Darkness* are examples of them. These are people whose normal ego seems to have dissolved away, and who don't experience any – or very little – psychological discord. Shifters have quiet minds, with little or no thought-chatter, and don't experience ego-isolation. Instead, they feel a strong sense of connection with other people, nature, and the world in general.

But we are jumping ahead of ourselves. Before we look into this state of harmony in detail, we have to journey deeper into the madness of the human mind, and the bizarre behavior it generates.

CHAPTER 4

The Madness of Elsewhereness

A couple of years ago I visited the British Museum in London, and came across a group of tourists who were filming the museum's exhibits with mobile phones and video cameras. They weren't actually *looking* at the ancient relics, just filming them. The museum was busy and some exhibits, such as the Rosetta Stone, were so popular that it was difficult for them to film without obstruction, so occasionally the tourists grew impatient with one another and started to jostle and push. (Of course, if they'd simply been content to *look* at the exhibits this wouldn't have been such a problem.) As I was observing the tourists, it struck me that *none of them are actually here now*. Rather than looking at these amazing relics now, I thought, they're only preparing to look at them in the future, when they get back home. In fact they're not visiting this museum now, they're visiting it in the future.

It seemed an absurd situation. Since they're physically here now, wouldn't it be easier for them to put the video cameras down and actually look at the exhibits now, rather than put if off until some future date? I thought. Wouldn't the actual *present* experience of seeing the Rosetta Stone – the full sensory experience of being here and now – be much more fulfilling than the experience of watching it on DVD at a later date?

About a year ago I witnessed a similar scene at a family wedding. The bride spent hours getting ready in the morning. Her friend (who worked as a hairdresser) styled her hair and she hired a professional beautician to do her makeup and nails. The actual marriage ceremony was quite short, and filmed by several different people on mobile phones and digital cameras. Later that afternoon, at the reception, the bride and groom spent most of their time walking around the grounds of the hall being photographed. They stopped underneath trees, by flowerbeds, by the gates of the hall, posing by themselves and then with a variety of combinations of family members. The process seemed to last forever, and to be the main focus of the reception.

And it made me wonder: is this wedding really taking place *now*? Had the bride spent so long getting ready because she wanted to look good for the ceremony, or because she wanted to look good in the *future*, when she watched the video of the ceremony and looked at the photos? As I watched them pose for photos, it struck me that the bride and groom weren't actually *here*. They were in the future, looking at these photos five, ten or 15 years from now. They were more interested in recording the day for the future then actually experiencing it now, in the present.

Again, I thought, wouldn't it be much better to forget about the future and give their full attention to the present experience of their wedding day, to live fully in the moment and take in the reality of what was happening in the now? Wouldn't that make a much more fulfilling wedding day?

These are extreme examples, but they're illustrations of one of the major effects of humania, although one that may not be immediately obvious: our inability to live in the present. As well as 'the people who can't do nothing,' an indigenous anthropologist might call us 'the people who can't live in the present.'

Terms like 'living in the present' or 'in the here and now' have become so familiar that they're almost clichés, but what do they actually mean?

Living in the present means being fully conscious of your experience, experiencing the is-ness of your surroundings, and of the sensations you're having. It means living in the world – as opposed to living inside your head – while being aware of yourself, in your own mental space.

You can live in the present when you have a shower in the morning; rather than letting your attention be immersed in thoughts, bring your attention to the sensations you're feeling right at this moment – the sensation of warm water splashing against your skin and running down your body. You can live in the present when you eat – instead of reading a newspaper or magazine or chatting to the person next to you while you eat, give your attention to the smell and taste of the food and the sensations of chewing and swallowing it. And you can live in the present while you're walking down the street, if you give your attention to the sensation of your feet touching and leaving the pavement, and really *look* at the buildings and the trees you pass, and the clouds and the sun above you.

This sounds simple, but it's something that most of us rarely do. Because of our ego-madness, we spend most of our lives in a state of absence, or 'elsewhereness.'

Elsewhereness

There are a number of ways in which humania takes us away from the present. On the one hand, our thought-chatter takes us 'elsewhere.' We can't experience the world directly through our senses, but only through a fog of mental impressions. Instead of being aware of the taste of your food, the sensation of water against your skin, or the buildings and other phenomena around you, you're in the bar with your friends last night, or ten years ago when your children were babies, or a few days in the future at a pop concert, or a few weeks in the future at a job interview you're dreading. This is what I sometimes call 'internal elsewhereness' – we're absent because our attention is immersed inside us, in our thoughts.

We're always aware of our surroundings *to a degree,* of course – if we weren't, we'd bump into walls, get run over or miss our train stop. But we're usually only aware of them in a rudimentary, automatic way. Every minute of the day is filled with different experiences – different sights and sensations, different feelings, tastes, smells and sounds – but we're only conscious of these to a very small degree. We aren't *completely* elsewhere, but we're usually only present to a very small degree. We travel without being really aware of our surroundings, look without really seeing, eat without really tasting, breathe and move without being conscious of our bodies.

And if we're not absent internally in this way, we're usually absent *externally,* by giving our attention to distractions and activities. At the same time as taking us out of ourselves, activities and distractions take us out of the present. To a greater or lesser extent – depending on *how* absorbed we become – when we watch TV, play computer games, or do our jobs, we narrow our attention down to one focus, and exclude the rest of our surroundings from our awareness, and also lose awareness of *ourselves.* Rather than being *here,* we're immersed in the alternate reality of TV shows or computer games, or in the abstract worlds of information we take in from magazines, newspapers or the Internet. This is what you might call 'external elsewhereness.'

In the modern world, 'external elsewhereness' is becoming easier and easier to access. A few years ago, there were some situations where it was hard to find – in waiting situations (e.g. at the bus stop, in the doctor's waiting room, or stuck in traffic), traveling on a train or a bus, or walking from one place to another. You could always read while you were waiting or traveling, but often the magazine or newspaper might not be interesting enough to hold your attention, so that it was easy to drift into 'internal elsewhereness' instead. Or you might even experience a touch of 'hereness' – or presence – and pay real attention to your surroundings, the people around you, the buildings you were passing, and the sky above you. But with the advent of gadgets like Blackberries, eBook readers, iPads, smart phones and iPods, there is instant, easy access to external elsewhereness in every situation. There's always an entertaining alternative to being aware of your surroundings and your experience. In many people's lives, reality is just an occasional presence, an incidental background to the endless parade of entertainment passing before their eyes. It's never been as easy to escape the present, and people have never been as alienated from it.

We often go through the whole day switching from internal to external elsewhereness, with our attention bouncing from one distraction or activity to the next, with short periods of thought-chatter in-between. It's quite rare that our attention becomes fully focused on the real physical world around us or on the sensations we're experiencing. It's quite rare that our attention withdraws into our own being, so that we really feel our presence in the world.

A lot of the time we aren't even present to the people we meet throughout the day. Often we don't give our full attention to our partners, friends, and family or to strangers when we talk to them. We might look at them and nod our heads every few seconds, but at the same time we're thinking about the e-mails we're going to write, or the new CD we're going to listen to later. This causes problems in our relationships, since it makes our partners, work colleagues and friends feel devalued. We're effectively saying to them, 'You're not worthy of my attention.'

Of course, there's nothing wrong with letting yourself be taken out of the present *sometimes*. We can't give our attention to our surroundings and our experience all the time. We need to narrow our attention to one focus a lot of the time to deal with the demands of everyday life, in order to concentrate and absorb information. The problem is that we spend almost no time in the present, or that we're only ever in the present to a very limited extent.

But hold on, you might object, what about when you *think* about the present?

But you can never think about the present, only experience it. When you drink a cup of tea, you can only experience it, not think about it. When you look at a beautiful landscape, you can only experience it, not think about it. If you *do* start thinking about it – for example, if you start comparing it to another landscape or wondering about the animals that might live there – you've already moved out of the present; you are no longer experiencing it fully. Thinking is never about the present, but always about the future or past. Your thought-chatter consists of replayed past experiences, anticipated future experiences, and more chaotically, random impressions and bits of information you've processed at some point in the past, or imaginary scenarios and situations that aren't part of the past, future or present, because they're unreal.

In a normal state of mind, you might ask yourself: what's the point in paying attention to my surroundings? I've seen trees, flowers, buildings, and everything else thousands of times before and there's nothing special about them. They're just ordinary and dreary.

But when you are truly present, you realize that you were never *really* seeing these things. The world becomes a completely different place, a much more beautiful, meaningful, and harmonious one, which we intuitively know is closer to the reality than our normal vision. The world around us comes to life, as if a new dimension has been added to it. The night sky outside your window seems to radiate benevolence, the trees sway with a beautiful serenity, and harmony pervades the air. It seems somehow magnificently right to be alive in the world. In this state of presence, you experience yourself in a completely different way too, with a new relationship to the cosmos, other people and to yourself. You feel a deep-rooted sense of inner wellbeing, a sense of inner fullness and stillness, together with a sense of connectedness to the world.

Looking forward

Another way in which we escape the present is by 'looking forward.' Because we often feel dissatisfied in the present, we turn our attention away from it, and take refuge in the future.

When I was at university, I suffered from depression. In the last year of my course, I lived alone in a single room and cut myself off from other people. I stopped going to lectures (I only went to two in the whole year) and only attended the bare minimum of seminars each week. I had one friend who I saw every week or two, but the rest of the time I was alone. I lost confidence in social situations, and felt as though I didn't know how to communicate anymore. I even found it difficult just to go into shops to buy food or cigarettes. I stayed up until the early hours of the morning, and usually got up around lunchtime.

I felt so unhappy that I decided I was going to leave university, even though it was only a few months before I finished my degree. I decided that I was going to go abroad. I told myself that in May, after saving up some money, I would go to Paris. I'd heard there was a bookshop there with lots of small rooms where you could live for free if you were a writer. Apparently all you had to do was turn up and hand over a piece of writing to the owner – if he was impressed he would let you stay above the shop. I'd written some poetry and had started a novel, and had a romantic image of myself as a novelist in Paris, like Henry Miller or Ernest Hemingway. It would mean leaving university without a degree, but what did that matter?

That was one idea. Another was that I was going to live as a busker in Amsterdam. I occasionally went busking in the town center, playing guitar and singing, even though I never made very much money. But I'd heard that Amsterdam was a busker's paradise, and that you could sleep on canal boats for a cheap price.

Looking back, there was no way on Earth I was going to carry out either of these plans. At that time I wouldn't have been brave enough to travel abroad on my own – I was too insecure and naive. I wouldn't have been foolish enough to leave university either, just before the end of the course, after three years. But in my mind it was clear. I remember telling someone about my plans and he looked at me doubtfully and said, 'You're one of those people who makes plans but doesn't go through with them, aren't you?' I was hurt and puzzled. I didn't understand what he meant. To me, there was no doubt that in a few months I'd be living off a couple of hours' singing a day and sleeping on a canal in Amsterdam, or writing short stories in the Parisian cafés.

And of course, I didn't do anything. I sat out the final months of my course, somehow scraped through my exams, and returned to my hometown to try to rebuild my personality and my life.

Eventually it occurred to me that I'd been using these pipedreams as a strategy to cope with my unhappiness. In a different environment, I might have tried to escape from my psychological discord by taking drugs or drinking. But instead I used imaginary futures to make my present seem more endurable.

The Iceman Cometh by the American playwright Eugene O'Neill expresses how vital pipedreams can be for human beings. The play is set in a rundown bar; the characters are tramps and alcoholics who cope with the hopelessness of their predicament by deluding themselves. One of them, Joe, once owned a casino and keeps saying that he's going to reopen it soon; Cecil 'The Captain' Lewis claims that any moment now he's going back to England to live; Pat McGloin, a former police lieutenant, tells the others that he's waiting for the right time to appeal against the charges that saw him kicked out of the force; 'Jimmy Tomorrow' is a former journalist who keeps saying that 'tomorrow' he's going to get a new job, and so on. But tomorrow never comes, of course, and they all exist in limbo, anticipating a reality that never comes into being.

Another character, a salesman called Hickey, appears at the bar once a year, on his return from his sales trips. He's recently stopped drinking and feels like a new man, free and contented. He tries to persuade the characters to stop dreaming and try to achieve their goals. 'Just stop lying about yourself and kidding yourself about tomorrows,' he tells them. The next day all the men dress up in their best clothes, and head out into the city, planning to look up old contacts and find jobs.

None of them have any success, of course, and they all come back to the bar that evening in a state of despair. After trying to achieve them, they realize how unfeasible their hopes were, and can't use them to help keep them sane anymore. They can't even find solace in drink now, and curse Hickey for showing them the truth. But then, after a few hours, the survival mechanism of 'looking forward' kicks in again. They go back to their drunken delusions, keeping faith in a tomorrow that never comes. The moral of O'Neill's play is that human beings need pipedreams for the same reason that Pascal believed we need diversions: to stop us facing up to the awful reality of our predicament.

Again, these are extreme examples, but it's a strategy that we all use frequently. It can happen so subtly that you may not consciously be aware of the process. You might be at work on a Wednesday afternoon, feeling a little bored, or watching TV on your own in the evening, feeling a little lonely. You react to these negative feelings by looking into the future and scanning for any upcoming events or arrangements you think you're going to enjoy. You instinctively need to 'latch on' to something in the future. At work, you might look forward to a drink or meal in the evening to get you through the day. Or during the week, you might look forward to a night out with friends at the weekend. You picture yourself there, enjoying the meal or chatting and laughing with your friends, and straightaway your mood perks up, and the time doesn't seem to weigh so heavily on your hands.

Or, if you can't find anything to latch on to in the future, you *create* something. You phone a friend and ask her if she wants to go out for a meal, you book a ticket for a concert or ask your partner if he fancies going away for the weekend next month. And so you do have something to look forward to, and there is some future happiness to distract you from your present discontent.

Most of us try to make sure that there's at least one pleasant future event at the back of our minds to which to turn our attention. It could be a favorite TV show, your football team's next home game, or your next vacation. Or, perhaps slightly less commonly, we give ourselves much more long-term aims to look forward to – a plan to give up your humdrum job in a couple of years and start your own business or go traveling around the world, or pipedreams of 'making it' as an actor or pop star – so that we can anticipate and imagine the lifestyles we'll have then.

However, one of the problems with the future is that at some point it always becomes the present – and it usually doesn't live up to our expectations. The night out or weekend away might be very pleasant, but somehow the reality wasn't quite as exhilarating as the anticipation. Often this is because when we arrive in the future, we always take our psychological discord with us. What you didn't include in your image of your weekend away was that you'd be carrying around exactly the same background anxiety in your mind as at home.

But in a way this doesn't matter, because as soon as one event passes, we replace it with another. Even if the TV show or football was disappointing, you can always look forward to tomorrow night or next Saturday. The whole point of 'looking forward' isn't to actually enjoy the event you anticipate, but to take you away from the present.

Many people 'wish away' their whole lives like this, switching their attention from one future event to the next. Almost as soon as they get back from one vacation, they book another and start telling their friends, 'I can't wait till I go to Peru – it'll be the best two weeks of my life.'

This is one of the ways that the teacher I knew – who I mentioned in Chapter 1 – dealt with her unhappiness. Since she had lots of time off school, she booked as many vacations and weekends away as she could afford. She would talk excitedly about the trips for weeks beforehand, spending hours shopping for new clothes. For some reason though, the trips always seemed to go wrong. The accommodation or the food would be terrible, she'd fall out with her partner, get irritated by her companions, or have an accident. But none of these experiences deterred her from looking forward to the next one as much as the last.

Of course, there's nothing wrong with looking forward to the future to a degree. If we know there are pleasant events in front of us, why shouldn't we anticipate them and feel happy about them? But the point is that for many of us 'looking forward' becomes a strategy of escaping from the present. If we were happy in the present – in other words, if we felt comfortable within our own mental space – we would be much less focused on the future.

Rushing away from the present

Look out on to a busy city street – you see masses people hurrying by, staring straight ahead with furrowed brows, zigzagging in and out of each other's way. They're rushing to get to meetings, to get home early, to get to the shops before they close, or just to get away from the stress of the city itself – but the destination they're really heading toward is the future. They're rushing away from the present, and into the future. When you rush, your mind is already in the future, and the present is just an inconvenience that stops you getting there.

Of course, a lot of the time we rush because we have no choice. Our lives are so hectic that we often struggle to keep up with our deadlines and appointments or to accomplish our daily tasks, and so we have to hurry to keep ourselves on track. But we often rush even though we don't need to, as another way of escaping from the present. We often find ourselves walking quickly even when there's time to spare, or rushing to eat a meal, to do the shopping in the supermarket or do the household chores even when there's no real time pressure on us at all. In these cases, rushing is a reaction to psychological discord. It's a sign that you feel dissatisfied, bored or frustrated. We reject the present because we feel uncomfortable in it.

Like the need for distraction, both the degree to which you need to rush and to look forward to the future are signs of how much discord there is inside you. If you observe yourself, you'll find that in moments when you're not disturbed by too much discord – when your mind is fairly quiet and you feel some contentment – you don't need to rush at all. You don't mind if your train is ten minutes late, or if you get stuck in traffic on the way home. In these moments the future has little relevance to you either. You may have all kinds of pleasant events coming up over the next few weeks, but you don't need to look forward to them. But when you feel most unhappy, you feel most impatient. You're desperate to escape the present, and any slight obstacle or delay increases your frustration and anger.

Hoping to live, but not living

As a very perceptive observer of human nature, Blaise Pascal was well aware of human beings' inability to live in the present. As he wrote,

> We are so unwise that we wander about in times that
> do not belong to us, and do not think of the only one
> that does; so vain that we dream of times that are not

*and blindly flee the only one that is... Thus we never
actually live, but hope to live.*[1]

Our lives consist of 80 or more years of constant flowing
present-ness – if we're lucky – but for almost all the time
we aren't *in* that flow. We swim against it, jump backward
into the past, forward into the future or across into alternate
realities. We live for 80 or more years, but in a sense we don't
really live, because we are not in the world, or in our own
being. Our lives only consist of the present, so if we're not
in the present we aren't really living. And if we spend all our
lives outside the present, we spend our whole lives not living.

However, the state of harmony and presence – where life
is revealed as a beautiful and meaningful adventure, and the
universe is revealed as a radiant and benevolent place – is
our natural state, our birthright as human beings. Later, in
Part II, we'll see how we can regain it.

CHAPTER 5

The Madness of Constant Wanting

In January 1848, a man named James Marshall was building a sawmill by a river near present-day Sacramento in the USA, when he saw an unusual piece of glowing metal on the floor. He took the metal to his employer, who tested it and confirmed it was gold. Within a few weeks, once rumors of the discovery had spread, tens of thousands of people were flocking to the area, struck by 'gold fever.' Ships were abandoned all over the Californian coast, businesses closed down, and whole towns became deserted. And once the news spread overseas – after the *New York Herald* picked up the story a few months later – a stampede of immigration from all over the world began. In a little over a year, San Francisco grew from a shantytown of 79 buildings to a city of tens of thousands. Over the next few years, at least 300,000 gold-seekers came to California.

Some early gold prospectors did well – the average amount of gold they found in a month was the equivalent of a year's typical salary. But as early as 1850, most of the easily accessible gold had gone, and the US Authorities had to take measures to stop new immigrants from taking what was left. Most prospectors who arrived after 1850 either made very little or actually lost money. Immigrant gold prospectors were taxed heavily, and some Americans began attacking foreigners.

The effect on California's Native Americans was catastrophic. They were driven from their traditional hunting and gathering grounds, and gravel, silt and toxic chemicals from the new mines polluted the rivers where they fished and drank. Some Indian groups used force to try to protect their lands, but were massacred by the miners. Those who weren't killed by the miners slowly starved to death, or died from diseases passed on by the immigrants. Others were kept as slaves, while attractive young women were kidnapped and sold. As a result, the Californian Native American population fell from around 150,000 in 1845 to 30,000 in 1870.

This savage materialism was typical of European immigrants' attitude to the 'New World' of America. They saw it as a treasure house of resources to ransack, and saw the indigenous population as an inconvenient obstacle to be eradicated.

For their part, the Native Americans had no interest in gold. Some of them knew where it was, but didn't bother digging for it. They weren't interested in accumulating wealth – they only worked as much as was necessary to keep themselves alive, and had no desire to collect valuable or beautiful objects.

The idea that you could own or buy any metals, land or any natural resources seemed bizarre to the Indians. As one Seneca chief said, 'A man cannot sell the land any more than he can sell the sea or the air he breathes.'[1]

Some tribes were so confused by the colonists' insatiable desire for gold that they believed that the metal must be a kind of deity with supernatural powers. Why else would they go to such lengths to get hold of it? When an Indian chief in Cuba learned that Spanish sailors were about to attack his island, he started to pray to a chest full of gold, appealing to the 'gold spirit' that he believed they worshiped. But the 'gold spirit' didn't show him any mercy – the sailors invaded the island, captured the chief, and burned him alive.[2]

Modern materialism

Nowadays, our materialism is just as rampant and destructive as the gold diggers', even if it's not so overt. In the modern world, the most destructive and naked materialism is undertaken not by ordinary people like the gold diggers, but by multinational companies – oil companies who destroy natural areas to drill and pollute the seas; agricultural corporations who chop down forests to grow their crops and use massive amounts of fertilizers and pesticides to make them grow; companies producing plastic goods that end up in the sea, killing or damaging marine life. The governments who allow them to do this are also to blame, of course, but before we blame multinational companies outright, it's important to remember that they're only able to do this because we, as individuals, want to consume their products. It's true that companies have to use advertisements to convince us that we need their products – or at least to persuade us to buy their variant instead of another company's – but still they and their products only exist because of a powerful acquisitive and materialistic urge inside *us*.

In fact, the gold prospectors' naked materialism was more forgivable than ours, since they were living in a time of great poverty, and for many of them gold mining offered an escape from starvation. But most of us in the Western, industrialized world don't have that excuse. Our appetite for wealth and material goods isn't driven by hardship, but by our inner discontent. We're convinced that we can buy our way to happiness, and that wealth is the path to permanent fulfillment and wellbeing. We still measure 'success' in terms of the quality and price of the material goods we can buy, or in the size of our salaries.

This association of happiness with wealth is so pervasive that, just like the gold prospectors, many people are willing to go to any length to become rich. Almost every day, there is a bizarre story in the newspapers about someone who commits a sickening crime in their pursuit of wealth. Just this morning I heard a report on the radio news about three generations of one family who lived together in the same house – a daughter, a mother and grandmother. When the grandmother died at 95, the daughter and mother didn't tell anyone, but left her body unburied in her bedroom. For six months, they pretended she was still alive, so that they could keep claiming her pension and other benefits.

In a story with some similarities, in 2008 a nine-year-old girl from Yorkshire called Shannon Matthews apparently went missing on her way home from school. The police staged a massive hunt for her, searching thousands of houses. Her mother appeared on TV, begging for help from the public. A fund was set up to help the search, and quickly reached £50,000, including a sizeable reward offered by a newspaper. But after 24 days, Shannon was found in her step-uncle's apartment, a mile away from her home. She had been kept drugged with sleeping pills and only allowed out for short periods, tied to a leash. It soon came to light that Shannon's disappearance had been a moneymaking plot devised by her mother and step-uncle. They were hoping to net the proceeds of the fund, including the reward.

Our mad materialism would be more understandable if there was evidence that material goods and wealth do lead to happiness. But there is no evidence of this. Study after study by psychologists has shown no correlation between wealth and happiness, except in cases of real poverty, when extra income does relieve suffering and brings security. But once our basic material needs are satisfied, our level of income makes little difference to our level of happiness. Research has shown, for example, that extremely rich people are not significantly happier than people with an average income, and suffer from higher levels of depression.[3] Researchers in positive psychology have concluded that true wellbeing does not come from wealth, but from other factors such as good relationships, meaningful and challenging jobs or hobbies, and a sense of connection to something bigger than us – such as a religion, a political or social cause, or a sense of mission.[4]

Explanations for materialism

Many economists and politicians believe that acquisitiveness – the impulse to buy and possess things – is natural to human beings. This seems to make sense in terms of Darwin's Theory of Evolution: since natural resources are limited, human beings have to compete over them, and try to claim as large a part as possible. It seems to make sense in terms of modern Neo-Darwinism too, or 'evolutionary psychology' – the controversial field that seeks to explain human nature in evolutionary terms. Since, according to these theories, the main driving force of human behavior is the genetic impulse to survive and reproduce, we're impelled to try to accumulate possessions and wealth because they increase our chances of survival. On the one hand, wealth increases our access to life-sustaining resources, and at the same time it makes men more attractive to women (who see them as a way of securing their own survival, and that of their children), and hence enhances their reproductive possibilities. After all, we're made up of 'selfish genes' that are determined to survive and replicate themselves at any cost. Wealth is a way of ensuring that they replicate themselves, and other sets of 'selfish genes' – ones unrelated to us – are rivals with whom we naturally compete.

One of the problems with this theory is that there is actually nothing 'natural' about the desire to accumulate wealth. In fact, this desire would have been disastrous for earlier human beings. For the vast majority of our time on this planet, human beings have lived as hunter–gatherers – small tribes who would usually move to a different site every few months. As we can see from modern hunter–gatherers, this way of life has to be non-materialistic, because people can't afford to be weighed down with unnecessary goods. Since they moved every few months, unnecessary goods would simply be a hindrance to them.

As I discussed in Chapter 2, most indigenous groups are very egalitarian too. Even when they do possess goods, hunter–gatherers share them with each other, rather than possess them individually. Apart from a few personal items used on a daily basis – such as cooking utensils and tools – the whole group shares everything. Sharing is seen as a moral imperative and personal possession potentially a crime, which potentially disturbs the balance and harmony of the group. So there's no question of the materialistic urge being a natural instinct inherited from our ancestors. If anything, it's *non*-acquisitiveness that is natural.

Another theory is that the restlessness and constant wanting that fuels our materialism is a kind of evolutionary mechanism keeping us in a state of alertness. (The psychologist Mihalyi Csikszentmihalyi has suggested this, for example[5]). Dissatisfaction keeps living beings on the lookout for ways of improving their chances of survival; if they were satisfied they wouldn't be alert, and other creatures would take the advantage.

But there is no evidence that other animals live in a state of restless dissatisfaction. On the contrary, many animals seem to lead very slow and static lives, content to remain within their niche and to follow their instinctive patterns of behavior. And if this behavior drives our materialism, we would probably expect other animals to be acquisitive too. But again, there is no evidence that – apart from some food hoarding for the winter months – other animals share our materialistic impulses.

In my view, acquisitiveness is best understood in psychological terms, as a consequence of humania. Animals and most indigenous peoples aren't materialistic simply because they don't suffer from our ego-madness.

Our mad materialism is partly related to our inner discontent. As I mentioned at the beginning of Chapter 3, because we feel uneasy and dissatisfied inside, we instinctively look to external things to try to alleviate our discontent. Materialism does give us a kind of happiness – the temporary thrill of buying something new and the ego-inflating thrill of owning it afterward. And we use this kind of happiness to try to override – or compensate for – the fundamental unhappiness inside us.

In addition, our desire for wealth is a reaction to the sense of lack and vulnerability generated by ego-separation. This generates a desire to makes ourselves more whole, more significant and powerful. We try to bolster our fragile egos and make ourselves feel more complete by accumulating wealth and possessions.

It doesn't work, of course – or at least, it only works for a very short time. The happiness of buying or owning a new item rarely lasts longer than a couple of days. The sense of ego-inflation generated by wealth or expensive possessions can be more enduring, but it's very fragile too. Your happiness depends on comparing yourself to other people who aren't as well off as you, and evaporates if you compare yourself to someone who is wealthier. And no matter how much we try to complete or bolster our ego, our inner discontent and incompleteness always re-emerges, generating new desires. No matter how much we get, it's never enough. You thought a four-bedroom house would satisfy you, but now you'd like an even bigger one. You thought that a six-figure salary would be more than enough to meet your needs, but after a couple of years you're aiming to increase it even more. You thought your house was exactly as you wanted it, but soon you're itching to buy an unnecessary new carpet, a fashionable new type of fridge, or the latest type of hi-fi equipment. As Buddhism teaches, desires are inexhaustible. The satisfaction of one desire just creates new desires, like a cell multiplying.

And still, after satisfying these endless desires, we're in the same state of discontent that we were before.

The madness of status-seeking

All of this applies to another way in which we seek happiness and fulfillment: through status, or its close relatives power, success and fame. Our desire for status is another way of trying to alleviate our innate sense of lack and insignificance. We try to reinforce the ego through power and success, to build ourselves up into significance to try to overcome the sense of insignificance inside us.

Status is the only commodity that can rival wealth in its appeal to human beings, and throughout history people have gone to extreme lengths to obtain it. In fact, wealth and status are so closely linked that they're the two main components of the 'happiness paradigm' of our culture. Happiness comes not only from obtaining as much material wealth as possible, but also from gaining as much status and power as possible. In addition to becoming wealthy, being a 'success' means becoming 'someone,' an important, respected person who 'makes their mark' on the world. If you go through life in a fairly low-paid job, driving an old car and living in a small house, and if you didn't 'excel' in any particular way or draw any attention to yourself, you're liable to be considered a 'failure.'

In earlier centuries, status was mainly about power. To be considered an 'important' person you had to get into a dominant position over other people, whose lives you could control, and who would treat you with deference (and in material terms, so that you could control resources and exploit others to increase your wealth). As a result, societies were always full of conflict, as people jostled and fought to get into positions of power, and as the oppressed rose up and rebelled against the powerful. For instance, in one 60-year period of Russian history, from 1801 to 1861, there were almost 1,500 revolts by serfs and peasants.

Today, at least in countries where power structures are fairly stable and egalitarian, most people try to gain status through success, achievement and fame. We try to become important by 'making it' in our chosen fields, climbing to the top of our career ladders, or by doing unusual or significant acts that will attract a lot of attention, like breaking a record, creating a work of art or a new invention. Or, in another connection between them, we might try to gain status through wealth, which enables us accumulate 'status symbols' such as designer clothes and expensive cars.

In recent times, fame in itself has become more attractive as a source of status. Whereas in the past people were likely to say they wanted to be famous *for* something (e.g. a famous dancer or singer or sports player) nowadays young people are more likely to say they *just* want to be famous. That is, they just want to be in the media spotlight, on TV or in the newspapers, so that they can be the center of attention and feel that they're 'someone,' that they're special and important. In a recent survey of more than 1,000 teenagers, for example, 54 percent said they wanted to be famous, compared to 15 percent who wanted a medical career and 13 percent who wanted to work in the media. Of those who said they wanted to be famous, 68 percent were unsure of exactly what they wanted to be famous for[6].

The madness of competition

The need for material wealth and status manifests itself in the absurd competitiveness of modern life. After all, there is only a certain amount of each of them to go around, so we have to fight against each other to get hold of them.

About 12 years ago, my wife and I moved to Singapore. Pam was working in a hospital, and I found a part-time job as an English teacher. In the beginning, we were open to the idea of living there permanently, but found Singaporean culture uncomfortably competitive. People were living as if a starting pistol had fired the moment they were born, as if there was a track of achievement in front of them along which they had to keep moving as fast as possible, making as much progress as possible before they died. I used to teach English to schoolchildren on Saturdays, from 8 a.m. to 1 p.m. ('Teach' isn't really the right word, as all I did was give them one practice test after the next, and go through the answers.) In addition to their five days of conventional schooling, it was common for children to have three or four hours of home tuition in the evenings, plus the weekends.

I felt sorry for the kids – some of them were as young as eight, and didn't seem to have any time to enjoy themselves. Once I said to my class, 'So when do you kids get to play?' They looked at me as if they had never heard the word before. After a few seconds one of them replied, 'I usually get to play for a couple of hours on Sundays.'

I was also shocked at the way that Singapore's economic growth would be announced on the radio: 'Hey, we've just heard that in the last quarter the economy has grown by nearly 5 percent!' the cheerful DJ would announce. 'And that's all because of you guys! So keep working hard and let's see if we can keep the growth going for the next quarter!' Some Singaporeans who we got to know couldn't understand Pam and I – as Westerners, they expected us to play the status game too. They were perplexed by our reluctance to power dress, the fact that we didn't have a car, and that I carried a rucksack instead of a briefcase.

When we got back to the UK, we felt relieved to be back in a more easygoing culture. But this monstrous competitiveness has certainly crept into British culture too, particularly over the last 15 years or so. At my children's school, I'm sometimes shocked by the desperation of some of the parents – usually the middle-class ones – to give their children a head start in the race for status and achievement. They pay for home tutoring, give them extra worksheets to do in the evenings, test them on their spellings on the way to school, and force them to read books meant for children years older. At the same time as putting pressure on them, this is teaching our children that life is all about *striving*, struggling to achieve more. It's teaching them that happiness is something to be earned in the future, rather than a natural condition to enjoy in the present. In addition, it's helping to create a hostile, non-empathic attitude to other people, encouraging children to think of them as rivals, competitors in the race for success.

As adults, many of us compete against each other to get better qualifications, better jobs, better promotion prospects, bigger houses, better cars, and more fashionable clothes. With each passing year, we need to feel that we've moved a little farther forward in the race for money and status, or that we're at least keeping up with the others. So we keep trying to gain new skills and qualifications, to improve our standard of living, to make our homes a little more luxurious.

One problem with this competition is that it *keeps accelerating.* As each competitor speeds up a little, all the others have to speed up too. In the absence of a consensus agreement for everyone to slow down or stay as they are, people keep increasing their speed and so force others to do the same. Anyone who relaxes is left behind. And as the speed increases, so does the stress.

What's the point of competing? Is there really any point to life, if our lives are nothing more than a scramble for achievement and status, if we live with furrowed brows and our eyes fixed ahead, never stopping to take in the meaning of what we're doing or to focus on the present?

And like wealth, status rarely satisfies us anyway. For some people, no matter how much success, power or fame they achieve, it's never enough. They don't reach a point where they think, *Okay, so I'm successful enough now, I may as well stop.* Conquerors have to keep on invading new countries, business moguls have to keep on taking over companies, and pop stars have to sell more and more records and conquer more markets. Some people may have the misfortune to reach the pinnacle of success or fame, the point at which there is nothing left for them to achieve – once this happens, there's usually a fall into lethargy and boredom. And this is because, again, status and power don't heal us *inside*. No matter how much we accumulate, the sense of lack and insignificance is still inside us, waiting to re-emerge.

CHAPTER 6
Collective Madness

The desires for wealth and status are even more dangerous and devastating when they are expressed collectively – that is, when groups of human beings act together to try to increase their wealth, power and prestige. This goes a long way to explaining some of the major social pathologies that humania gives rise to, such as warfare, social inequality and oppression, and male domination.

The main motivation of warfare is the desire of one group of human beings – usually governments, but often the general population of a country, tribe or ethnic group – to increase their power and wealth. The group tries to do this by conquering and subjugating other groups, and by seizing their territory and resources. Pick almost any war in history and you'll find some variant of this cause: wars to annex new territory, to colonize new lands, to take control of valuable minerals or oil, to help build an empire to increase prestige and wealth, or to avenge a previous humiliation that diminished a group's power, prestige and wealth. One of the root causes of World War II was the humiliation of Germany after World War I, when the Treaty of Versailles punished them severely. The Germans were forced to give up large parts of their territory and pay billions of dollars in reparations, causing massive hardship. The aim of these measures was to ensure that Germany would never become a military power again, but it had the opposite effect, of course. The sense of humiliation gave rise to an intense desire to regain power and prestige, which developed into the 'Thousand Year Reich' envisioned by the Nazis.

Until the nineteenth century, European countries were at war with one or more of their neighbors, on average, nearly every second year. Between 1740 and 1897 there were 230 wars in Europe, and countries were almost bankrupting themselves with their military expenditure. (At the end of the eighteenth century the French government was spending two-thirds of its budget on the army, while Prussia was spending 90 percent.) Wars were shorter and less frequent during the twentieth century, but more advanced killing technologies meant that the death toll rose sharply. Whereas it is estimated that 'just' 30 million people died in all the European wars between 1740 and 1896, the combined death toll of the two World Wars was around 75 million.[1]

Warfare is so common to human beings that there's a tendency to think of it as normal and natural – and, indeed, there have been attempts to explain it in crudely biological or genetic terms. For example, warfare has been linked to a higher level of testosterone in men or a lower level of serotonin, both of which are associated with aggressive behavior.[2] There's no doubt, however, that even if there is some genetic or biological disposition toward aggression in human beings (although I believe that even this has been exaggerated), this tendency is massively intensified by humania. Far from being natural, war is a symptom of our insanity. Think of the European countries of the eighteenth and nineteenth centuries: groups of people who spoke very similar languages, who were often ethnically related, but who allowed generations of their young men to be killed, and generations of women and children to suffer poverty and starvation, in an endless struggle over land, wealth, prestige, and power. Think of the perverted ideology of militaristic cultures – such as ancient Sparta, nineteenth-century Prussia and early twentieth-century Japan – which held that killing other human beings (and sacrificing your own life in the process) was a noble and even moral act. Think of the bizarre philosophy of Social Darwinism – advocated by the Nazis and British colonialists – which held that warfare and colonialism were natural and right, since they were an enactment of the laws of survival, part of the evolutionary process by which the 'fittest' and strongest conquered and killed those who were weaker.

Social oppression and inequality

Another pathological characteristic of most human societies throughout history – and another consequence of the drive to gain power and wealth generated by humania – has been massive inequality and oppression. The great majority of human beings have always been, effectively, the slaves of a tiny minority who owned and controlled resources. If you had the misfortune to be born in Europe in the Middle Ages – or in Ancient Egypt, feudal Japan or China or any other society with a feudal system – the vast likelihood is that you would have been born into the life of a peasant or serf. As a serf, you would be little more than a slave. Your master would own the land on which you worked, and you couldn't leave it without his permission. He could transfer you to a different estate, while taking over your property and family. You could be called up to go to war at any time, leaving your crops to rot and your family to starve. It's also very possible that your master would beat you, punish you brutally for trivial crimes or – if you were a woman – rape you.

If you were slightly more fortunate, you might be born as a peasant, who rented his land from a landowner. But your predicament would still be dismal. Your landlord would most likely exploit you massively, charging you a high rent, in addition to taxes and compulsory 'gifts.' The church would want their share of your income too, in the form of tithes, or – if you didn't have any money – a share of your produce. Your house would be made of wood, mud, and manure, and life would be a constant struggle to survive, with very little water and food and no heating. You would be chronically malnourished, and in constant danger of starving altogether, especially in winter. And on top of all that, you would live in constant fear of being falsely accused of crimes, and being tortured and killed as a punishment. Brutal punishment – and the power of making the accusations that led to it – was one of the methods used by nobles and lords to keep their peasants under control.

On the other hand, if you were born into the aristocracy, or as a member of the nobility or gentry, you would effectively have won the lottery. You might own thousands of peasants or serfs – some Russian nobles in the nineteenth century owned 300,000 serfs – and you would probably consider yourself a higher human type than them, almost a member of a different species. You would think of your peasants as closer to animals than human beings (in estate records, it was not unusual for peasants to be listed as 'livestock' along with pigs and sheep). Your class would make up less than 10 percent of the population, but own practically all of the country's wealth and resources, and have complete control over all its laws and its government. There was no need for you to work, as the food, goods and money you extorted from your peasants or serfs would subsidize a lavish lifestyle. You would be exempt from punishment for most crimes and your life expectancy would be up to 20 years longer than your peasants.

If you were born of peasant stock in Europe during the nineteenth century your predicament would be even worse. After the Industrial Revolution, you would no longer be the slave of a lord or noble, but of a factory, mill or mine owner. You would work harder and live in even greater squalor, while the industrialists prospered just as much as the nobles. But at least the Industrial Revolution had the effect of breaking up the old feudal system, as a new middle class of businessmen took over from the nobility and gentry. Even so, in the UK, the laws and structures of societies were so weighted in favor of the privileged minority that it took decades of protest and campaigning – by groups such as the Chartists and Trade Unions – to slowly erode away the inequalities.

But of course, massive inequality still exists – most notably, on a global scale. When we consider the distribution of wealth and resources throughout the world as a whole, the inequalities are, if anything, even more grotesque than those of feudal societies hundreds of years ago. The richest 1 percent of the world's population owns 40 percent of its wealth, while 50 percent of the population owns just 1 percent. At the same time, 80 percent of people live on less than $10 per day, over 1 billion people don't have access to adequate water, and 2.5 billion people lack basic sanitation.[3]

The oppression of women

Even when they belonged to higher social classes, throughout history most women have effectively been slaves too. Until recent times, women in Europe, the Middle East and Asia were unable to have any influence over the political, religious or cultural lives of their societies. They couldn't own property or inherit land and wealth and were frequently treated as mere property themselves. In some countries moneylenders or tax collectors could confiscate women to help settle debts (this was, for example, a common practice in Japan from the seventh century CE onward.) In ancient Assyria, the punishment for rape was the handing over of the rapist's wife to the husband of his victim, to use as he desired. Most gruesome of all, some cultures practiced what anthropologists have called 'ritual widow murder' (or 'ritual widow suicide'), when women would be killed (or kill themselves) shortly after the death of their husband. This was common throughout India and China until the twentieth century, and there are still occasional cases nowadays.

Even in the so-called 'enlightened' society of Ancient Greece – where the concept of democracy supposedly originated – women had no property or political rights, and were forbidden to leave their homes after dark. Similarly, in Ancient Rome women were unable to take part in social events (except as employed 'escort girls'), and were only allowed to leave their homes with their husband or a male relative.

In Europe the status of women has risen significantly over the last few decades, but in many parts of the world male domination and oppression continue. In many Middle Eastern countries, for example, women effectively live as prisoners, unable to leave the house unless in the company of a male guardian. (Many Saudi Arabian women have only left their houses a handful of times in their whole lives.) And when – or if – they do go outside, they are obliged to cover themselves from head to toe in black, leaving them in danger of vitamin D deficiency and dehydration. They have no role at all in determining their own lives. They are seen as nothing more than a commodity, property of the males of the family, and as owners the men have the right to make decisions on their behalf. Their male owners have the right to have sex with them on demand too. In Egypt, surveys have shown that the vast majority of men and women believe it is acceptable for a man to beat his wife if she refuses sex[4].

Again, there have been attempts to explain the oppression of women in crude biological terms. For example, in *The Inevitability of Patriarchy*, the sociologist Stephen Goldberg suggests that men are naturally more competitive than women because of their high level of testosterone. This makes them aggressive and power-hungry, so that they inevitably take over the high-status positions in a society, leaving women to take the more subordinate roles[5].

There is no doubt, however, that this maltreatment of women is pathological, and another symptom of our underlying insanity. It's one thing to take over the positions of power in a society, but another to seemingly *despise* women, and inflict so much brutality and degradation on them. What sane species would treat half of its members

– and the very half who *gives birth* to the whole species – with such contempt and injustice? Despite their high level of testosterone, the men of many ancient and indigenous cultures revered women for their life-giving and nurturing role, so why don't we?

The oppression of women stems from men's desire for power and control. The same need that drives them to try to conquer and subjugate other groups or nations, and to oppress other classes or groups in their own society, drives them to dominate and oppress women. Since men feel the need to gain as much power and control as they can, they *steal away* power and control from women. They deny women the right to make decisions, so that they can make them for them; leave women unable to direct their own lives so that they can direct their lives for them. Ultimately, they're trying to increase their sense of significance and status, in an effort to offset the discontent and sense of lack created by humania.

The madness of honor

One of the most disturbing and pathological cultural practices generated by humania is 'honor killing' – the killing of relatives (the vast majority of them female, and in most cases young daughters) who have 'dishonored' the family. This practice is still prevalent in many Middle Eastern and Asian societies – not coincidentally, the same societies that are most oppressive toward women.

Honor killing is linked to the fear of losing status, and the desire to *protect* it. In the societies where it occurs, there is a pathological insecurity, a constant pressure to adhere to strict social conventions for fear of losing face, and of being ostracized by the rest of the community. (In this sense, it's linked to social identity and the need for belonging which we're going to examine in the next chapter.)

The women of the family are seen as representing its honor, so there is massive pressure on them to behave 'properly.' This means dressing modestly, not talking to men outside the family, never attracting attention to themselves, and most importantly of all, avoiding sex before marriage (or outside marriage, once they are wed) and agreeing to marry a partner chosen by their family. Other types of behavior seen as 'dishonorable' for women – and therefore as punishable by death – include political activism, investigating other religions, and requesting a divorce. There have also been many cases of homosexual boys being killed to preserve the family 'honor.'

If a family member deviates from this code of behavior, the family's reputation is sullied. The only way they can redeem themselves is by murdering the relative – again, usually the daughter – who has dishonored them. It doesn't matter if the relative is completely innocent. It could simply be that she's attractive, and so has been shown attention by men outside the family; it could be that she lost her virginity by being raped. The fact that she has sullied the family's reputation is enough to justify murdering her. Amnesty International reported a case in Turkey of a 16-year-old girl who was murdered after her family heard a love song being dedicated to her on the radio. In Pakistan, a girl with learning difficulties was killed after being raped, even though the relative who raped her was prosecuted.[6]

The United Nations has estimated that around 5,000 honor killings take place each year, but since many occur in isolated rural areas and aren't reported to authorities, it's likely that the real figure is much higher. In many countries, the practice is so socially acceptable that murderers are treated leniently, or not punished at all. In countries like Pakistan and Yemen, for example, police and prosecutors often ignore the killings. In Syria, the legal code states that if a man catches a female relative having illicit sex with another man and kills them (either just the woman or the partner as well), he is entitled to a reduced penalty of just two years in prison.

As I hinted above, honor killings are clearly related to male domination and low female status. It's only possible for fathers to kill their own daughters – or brothers their own sisters – because they place a very low value on female life. If women were revered and respected, then no one would consider killing – or even abusing – them. It's no coincidence that many of the cultures that practice honor killing – for example, India and Pakistan – also practice female infanticide. In these cultures, female life has negligible value, and so to destroy it is only a minor crime.

By any objective standards of behavior, it seems incredible and insane that parents are prepared to murder their own children – or brothers their own sisters – for the sake of status and reputation. It's also incredible that most honor killings are a punishment for completely natural and healthy human instincts: the 'crime' of falling in love with a member of a different caste (which is often the cause of honor killings in India), or with a stranger not handpicked by your parents, or the 'crime' of feeling sexual attraction and following this through to sex itself. Again, it's no coincidence that honor killings occur in societies that, in addition to being strongly patriarchal, have a high degree of sexual repression, and a neurotically hostile attitude to sex and the human body.

The lack of empathy

Although it's propelled by the desire for wealth and status, all of the brutality described above is only made possible by another major effect of humania: a reduced ability to empathize with other people.

Empathy is the ability to 'feel with' another person, to identity with them and sense what they're experiencing. It's sometimes seen as the ability to 'read' other people's emotions, or the ability to imagine what they're feeling, by 'putting yourself in their shoes.' In other words, empathy is seen as a *cognitive* ability, along the same lines as the ability to imagine future scenarios or to solve problems based on previous experience. But in my view empathy is more than this: it's the ability to make a psychic and emotional connection with another person, to actually *enter into* their mind-space. When we experience real empathy or compassion, our identity actually merges with another person's. The separateness between you and the other person fades away. Your 'self-boundary' dissolves so that in a sense – or to an extent – you *become* them.

However, our strongly developed ego makes it difficult for us to experience this state of connection. It 'walls us off' from other people, particularly those belonging to other groups – the other gender (in the case of female oppression), other tribes, and nations, races or classes. (We'll look at the importance of group identity in more detail in the next chapter.) The ego encloses us in a narrow world of our own thoughts and desires, making us so self-absorbed that it's difficult for us to experience the world from other people's perspective. Other people become truly 'other' to us. And this makes it possible for us to inflict suffering on them, simply because we can't *sense* the pain we're causing them. We can't feel with them enough to sense their suffering.

If you identify with another person, if you have a psychic and emotional connection with them, then it's impossible to treat them brutally. You recoil from their experience of suffering in the same way that you recoil from your own suffering. In fact, you feel a strong desire to *relieve* their suffering and aid their development. But if you can't identify with them, then there's no limit to the amount of suffering you can inflict. You can't sense their pain, so there's nothing to stop you causing it.

This is the major characteristic of psychopaths. They are completely unable to empathize and see the world from other people's perspective. They are completely self-absorbed and self-obsessed. The whole world, and the rest of the human race, only exists to serve their own desires. Of course, I'm not trying to say all human beings are psychopaths. It's a question of degree. Psychopaths are people who experience this lack of empathy and self-absorption at an extreme level. But it's there to some degree in all of us, especially men. Humania includes an element of psychopathy.

In other words, 'Man's inhumanity to man' has two fundamental causes: the desire for wealth and power, and the reduced capacity to empathize. These two factors have propelled most of the terrible suffering, misery and violence that run through recorded history.

Women and empathy

It's significant that research has shown that women generally appear to have a higher level of empathy than men. For example, studies have shown that women's friendships tend to be based on mutual help and problem sharing, whereas men usually develop friendships based on shared interests, such as sports and hobbies[7]. Men and women have also been shown to have different speaking styles. Conversations among women usually last longer, because of their use of more 'back-channel support,' such as nodding, smiling and other gestures. If they disagree, women tend to express their opinion indirectly rather than making a statement, helping to avoid confrontation. On the other hand, men tend to more blunt and opinionated. They use more imperatives and tend to 'talk over' other people more. As the psychologist Simon Baron-Cohen puts it, 'men spend more time using language to demonstrate their knowledge, skill and status.'[8] Studies have also shown that women are significantly better at gauging people's emotions purely from looking at their eyes[9].

This makes sense: after all, the vast majority of 'man's inhumanity' throughout history really has been *man's*. Almost all wars have been orchestrated and fought by men, and most social oppression has been inflicted by high-status men, seeking to protect and increase their power and wealth. (You could argue that this is partly because women were never able to get into positions of power, and so were never *able* to wage war or oppress people. But the reason for this, of course, was that men denied women access to positions of power in the first place, because of their own desire for them.)

This also makes sense in terms of women's role as mothers. Surely their nurturing role encourages empathy, because of the need for a strong emotional connection to children. At the very least, you could say that this emotional connection would have made it more difficult for women to lose the ability to empathize.

If it is true that women have a greater capacity for empathy, this suggests that they generally experience less ego-separation than men. After all, if they have a greater ability to 'feel with' other people, this can only be because they are less 'walled off' inside their own mental space. And since ego-separation is one of the main characteristics of humania, does this mean that women are less affected by the condition than men?

This would be a controversial conclusion, but I think there may well be some truth in it. Even so, it's only a case of suffering from a *slightly* milder case of the condition. Women still experience some degree of ego-isolation, of course, and they certainly do experience at least the same degree of cognitive discord as men. Women are mad too, even if they might not be quite as mad as men.

The madness of environmental destruction

There is a further collective pathology that relates to the issues we've looked at in this chapter: our suicidal destruction of our planet's life support systems. To an independent observer, this would be the final proof – if any were needed – that human beings suffer from a psychological disorder. Would a sane species be destroying the Earth's plant and animal life so wantonly, and filling the air and seas with such massive amounts of poisonous chemicals? Would they be consuming natural resources so rapaciously, at the same time as tearing up the Earth's surface in search of more? Would a sane species allow catastrophic trends like global warming, water shortage and overpopulation to intensify without taking any serious measures against them?

Indigenous peoples were in no doubt that our attitude to nature was pathological, and would lead to disaster. They have been consistently appalled by our lack of respect for the natural world, and systematic abuse of nature. Over 150 years ago Chief Seattle compared the white man to 'a stranger who comes in the night and takes from the land whatever he needs.' With great foresight, he warned President Franklin Pearce that his people 'will devour the Earth and leave behind only a desert.'[10] More recently, the Australian Aborigine Anne-Pattel Grey has complained of European Australians 'raping, murdering and abusing their Mother Earth,' and warned of the 'price they would pay for abusing [her].'[11]

Indigenous peoples respect nature because they sense that it's alive and because they feel connected to it. They sense that all natural things – not just animals but plants, stones, and the whole Earth itself are not just objects, but *beings,* who are part of the same web of creation as them. They *empathize* with plants, animals and the Earth, and so are reluctant to damage or destroy them. As the great Native American philosopher Luther Standing Bear wrote of the Lakota Indians, 'Kinship with all creatures of the earth, sky, and water was a real and active principle. In the animal and bird world there existed a brotherly feeling that kept the

Lakota safe among them.' This meant that, for the Lakota, in anticipation of the modern animal rights movement:

> *'The animals had rights – the right of a man's protection, the right to live, the right to multiply, the right to freedom, and the right to man's indebtedness – and in recognition of these rights the Lakota never enslaved an animal, and spared all life that was not needed for food and clothing.'*[12]

This attitude brought a sense of responsibility. Many indigenous peoples saw – and still see – themselves as the caretakers of nature, with a responsibility to preserve harmony. As Chief Edward Moody of the Nuxalk Nation says, 'We must protect the forests for our children, grandchildren, and children yet to be born. We must protect the forests for those who can't speak for themselves such as the birds, animals, fish and trees.'[13]

On the one hand, our environmental destruction is the direct result of the separateness of the ego. In the same way that this separateness makes it difficult for us to empathize with other people – especially members of other groups – it makes it almost impossible for us to empathize with natural things, or with the Earth itself. It means that we experience a sense of 'otherness' to nature, that we can't sense its aliveness and so don't feel any qualms about exploiting and abusing it.

Or on a wider scale, our ego-separateness means that we don't feel connected to the web of creation. As a result, we don't feel a responsibility to the rest of the web, or a duty to preserve its harmony. Instead, our separateness makes us feel entitled to *dominate* the rest of nature. This is why we feel entitled to *own* land and natural resources, which is one of the traits that indigenous peoples found most difficult to understand. Ownership implies a position of superiority and dominance. Since we know that *we* are conscious and alive ourselves, and perceive natural phenomena as *not* being alive and conscious, we feel that we're superior to nature, as a master is to a slave, and so feel entitled to dominate it. But indigenous peoples' sense of the sacredness and aliveness of nature means that they could never take this attitude. Even as communities, they rarely see themselves as owning land or natural resources in the sense that we understand the term.

In this sense, our abuse of the environment is propelled by the same need for power that makes us strive for influential positions. We seek power over nature, to dominate and oppress it, in the same way that we've always striven to oppress other groups, classes or castes. Instead of feeling the kinship that Luther Standing Bear described, we've traditionally seen nature – and all natural things – as an enemy to be conquered, something wild to be tamed and harnessed. In a fundamental way, our oppression of nature – mostly a male enterprise – is closely linked to the oppression of women. Nature is usually described in feminine terms – for example, Mother Nature, or the womb of the Earth – and women have traditionally been seen as the embodiment of nature, linked to creation through childbirth and powerful natural processes such as menstruation and lactation. And throughout history, the male ego has felt the need to have dominion over both of them.

Our desire for material goods is an important factor too. The Earth is the source of everything material – everything we produce and consume is made from it, and returns to it in some form. If we didn't have such a massive appetite for possessions, pleasures and status symbols, there would be much lower levels of both consumption and environmental damage.

And of course, overpopulation is another important factor. Naturally, the collective effects of humania intensify with numbers. One thousand years ago, with a population of only a few hundred million, there was a limit to the amount of damage the human race could do the biosphere, and to other species. But now that there are billions of mentally disordered individuals – billions of 'humaniacs' – wandering over the surface of this planet, it's not surprising that its future is in jeopardy.

CHAPTER 7
The Fragile Self

A couple of years ago, a friend of my wife spent weeks organizing the office Christmas party. She booked the room, organized the entertainment and tickets and sent out the e-mails. The party went well and at its end, her manager stood up to make the customary speech. But he didn't bother to thank her, which enraged her, after all the effort she had put in. 'Right,' she told herself, 'if he doesn't value my work, I'm not going to value him either.' From that point, she was difficult and uncommunicative to the manager, and their working relationship deteriorated so much that she ended up leaving the company – a mistake, she realized later, as she had been happy in the job.

A few years ago I was shocked to read a newspaper story about a high-speed shooting. A man in a sports car was so incensed at being overtaken by another fast car that he sped after it, drove alongside, pulled out a gun and started shooting at the driver. Luckily he didn't hit him.

In a less intense form, this type of road rage is very common. A number of people – usually men – have told me that they fly into a rage when anyone dares to overtake them, and chase after the driver, trying to get in front again. As my wife's friend did with her manager's ignorance, they interpret being overtaken as an insult, feeling devalued and disrespected.

These stories highlight another symptom of humania: the fact that human beings are so vulnerable to *slights*. It's all too easy for us to take offence – and feel emotionally wounded – if someone appears to disrespect us. Think about how you feel when someone forgets your birthday, or doesn't return your phone calls; or when you're not invited to a party or aren't included in an important meeting at work. We often like to think of ourselves as altruistic, willing to offer help freely, but think about how slighted you feel when you give someone a ride or cook them a meal, and they leave without saying thank you.

Watch yourself closely and you'll probably find that you feel slighted in one of these ways almost every day – possibly even several times a day. Maybe a person didn't give you any eye contact when you spoke to them, or pushed in front of you when you were standing in line. Perhaps you experienced rejection of some form, when your report was sent back for some more work, or a friend turned down an invitation.

Psychologists call these types of slights 'narcissistic injuries.' Ultimately, they all stem from the same basic sense of being devalued or disrespected.

The dangers of slighting

Slights may seem trivial, but they can have dangerous consequences. They can play on our minds for days, opening up psychological wounds that are difficult to heal. We replay the situation over and over again, until the hurt and humiliation eats away at us inside. This usually leads to an impulse to fight back, to avenge the damage to our self-esteem. This could mean slighting the person back: 'She didn't invite me to her party, so I'm not sending her a birthday card,' or 'He didn't thank me, so I'm going to ignore him from now on.' A grudge may develop: you end up looking the other way when you pass the person on the street, or making bitchy comments behind their back. And if the person reacts to your resentment, it could end up in a full-scale feud. A good friendship could dissolve into acrimony; a close family could needlessly fall apart.

Even more dangerously, especially with young men, slights can trigger a violent reaction. Criminologists have noted that many acts of violence stem from a sense of slight. The psychologists Martin Daly and Margo Wilson estimated that two-thirds of all murders were the result of men feeling that they had been disrespected and acting to save face.[1] In recent years, in the USA there has been a disturbing rise in the number of 'flashpoint killings' – casual murders triggered by trivial confrontations. In most cases, the flashpoint killer is a young man who becomes furious after feeling that he's been slighted in front of friends.

In one case, a teenager shot a man at a basketball match, because 'I didn't like the way he was eyeballing me.' He went up to the man and asked, 'What are you looking at?' This led to insults and the shooting. Another young man became enraged after an acquaintance tried to shake his hand while he was eating, and shot him later outside the café. One young woman stabbed another because she wore her dress without asking.[2]

It's not a coincidence that a large proportion of these sorts of crimes are related to alcohol. Most murders, manslaughters, and stabbings are committed under the influence of alcohol, as are around half of domestic assaults.[3]

This is partly because of alcohol's 'disinhibiting' effect; it's more difficult for us to control our impulses, including any aggressive ones. Alcohol also narrows our attention, so that we're more likely to misinterpret other people's behavior, and don't consider the consequences of violent acts.

However, perhaps the *primary* cause is that alcohol has the effect of inflating a person's self-esteem. When they're drunk, most people often feel more self-important and become more self-assertive. As a result, they're more sensitive to slights and insults. And because of the factors mentioned above – their weaker impulse control and narrower range of attention – they're very likely to respond to this perceived disrespect with violence.

This vulnerability to being slighted is another consequence of our ego-separateness. It's the result of the basic of sense of insecurity and insignificance that ego-separateness generates. Our ego is tiny and flimsy in the face of the enormous world 'out there,' like a tiny wooden beach shack at the edge of a vast ocean. We feel dwarfed by the sheer weight of the phenomena and events taking place 'out there.' How can we possibly have any significance in relation to them? How can this fragile entity inside our heads stand up to the might of the world?

As a result, the ego needs to be continually boosted by affirmation, attention and respect from others. We need to be shown that we're important. A slight can be a terrible blow because it uncovers our latent sense of insignificance.

The French psychologist Jacques Lacan put forward a similar explanation of aggression. He pointed out that most acts of aggression are the result of a threat to identity. As children, we're a collection of different desires and different biological processes that we have no control over. As we become adults we have to bring all these processes into a unity, to develop a coherent identity. When people offend or insult us, it makes us feel fragmented again and we react by striking out, as a way of reasserting our power and identity.[4]

The need for identity and belonging

This fragility and incompleteness of the ego also manifests itself in a desire to belong, to become part of a larger group identity, so that we can feel stronger and more secure.

This need to belong to a group is one of the hallmarks of adolescence. During adolescence, the ego rapidly develops as a structure, creating a sense of 'inner-ness' and separating us from the world. As a result, adolescents have a very fragile sense of self, which means that they're more vulnerable to feeling belittled by perceived slights and therefore more likely to commit violent 'slight crimes.' This is also why young people often have a need to *shock*, by wearing outrageous clothes and hairstyles, committing acts of vandalism, drinking too much or taking drugs. They are trying to assert their fragile identity and at the same time trying to gain attention to bolster their identity.

This also explains why teenagers have such a strong need for belonging. They need to reinforce their identity by being a part of a group or gang. It's massively important for them to be *accepted* by their chosen group and so they're willing to go to any lengths to 'fit in', subsuming their own identity within the group and following its fashions and codes of behavior. There is nothing worse than being 'left out' or ostracized, which means being left alone with their fragile selves, without external support.

When I was as at university in the late 1980s, it was fashionable to be a 'Goth.' Goths wore heavy black clothes with big black boots, dyed their hair black and listened to bands like The Cure and Siouxsie and the Banshees. They tried to avoid going out in the sunlight or being seen smiling or laughing. There was one bar in the Students' Union where they congregated; if any non-Goths strayed in by mistake, they would stare hard at them, letting them know they weren't welcome. Some of them wouldn't even talk to non-Goths. I liked a lot of the same music as the Goths – my favorite bands were Joy Division and The Doors – but I could never bring myself to dress in black clothes and become a member of their tribe. As a result, if ever I tried to be friendly to them – for example, by asking 'What's your favorite Joy Division song?' – they muttered noncommittally and turned away.

There was a girl on my course who looked very conventional when she first arrived, with brightly colored blouses and skirts and long fair hair. But one day, a few weeks later, I was shocked when she arrived at a lecture dressed as a Goth. She must have made an overnight decision to join the tribe: she'd dyed her hair jet black, and was suddenly wearing a long black skirt and heavy black boots. I couldn't help asking, 'What's happened to you?' She looked embarrassed and told me, 'Nothing – I just bought some new clothes.'

This explains how fashion works too, and why it's so important to teenagers. Fashion designers – and fashion magazines and major stores – exploit young people's need for belonging and status by telling them that a certain style is 'in' over the next few months. Once the style has been established, young people feel they have to wear that type of clothes (no matter how strange) for fear of being 'left out.' Sometimes I suspect that fashion designers are having a competition to see how far they can go before young people suddenly rise up and say 'Hold on – we're not wearing these ridiculous clothes!' At the time of writing, there's a trend for teenage boys to wear their jeans hanging down low, with the waist dangling around their thighs, exposing their underpants. It means that they can only walk with a slow swagger – which is probably part of the appeal. A few years ago I remember commenting to a friend, 'Fashions are getting so absurd that in a while it's going to fashionable to wear clothes inside out.' Lo and behold, a couple of years later, it did become a fashion to wear T-shirts with the inside hem on the outside. I also said to my friend, 'And the next fashion after that will be for men to wear underpants on their heads,' but that one hasn't come into being... yet.

Although it isn't as overt in adults, the need for belonging stays with us throughout our lives. For men, it often manifests in the urge to support a sports club: in the UK, usually a football club; in the USA, usually a baseball or American football team. Supporting a sports team provides a sense of group identity, a sense of being part of a tribe, in allegiance with thousands of others. There are other benefits too, of course: always having something to look forward to (the next match), a sense of purpose and mission (to win matches and trophies), and the exhilaration of being part of a crowd on match days. But this sense of group identity and belonging is probably the main psychological need that supporting a club satisfies.

More collective madness: group identity, moral exclusion, and conflict

More dangerously, this need for belonging and identity manifests itself in ethnicism, nationalism or religious dogmatism. It encourages us to cling to the identity of our ethnic group, country or religion, and to feel a sense of pride in being 'British,' 'American,' 'White,' 'Black,' 'Christian,' 'Muslim,' 'Protestant' or 'Catholic.' The problem with this isn't so much having pride in *our* identity, but the attitude this engenders toward *other* groups. Identifying exclusively with a particular group automatically creates a sense of rivalry and enmity with other groups. It creates an 'in–out group' mentality. Members of your group are given preferential treatment – they are your 'brothers' or 'sisters,' and you feel loyalty and compassion for them. But there is a tendency not to think of people in other groups as individuals anymore, but in generic terms, so that it's easy to apply prejudice to them. Other groups become rivals, and are seen as threats to your identity. Your group has a need to feel superior to other groups – in order to strengthen its identity further – and is likely to denigrate and disrespect the 'others' in order to do so.

Another attraction of group identity, besides this sense of belonging, is that gives us a label to define ourselves with. It enables us to 'be' a 'Goth,' a 'Manchester United fan,' a 'socialist' or a 'Christian.' This is another way in which groups strengthen our sense of identity. If you ask yourself the question 'Who am I?' you have another ready answer, in addition to other labels such as 'husband/wife', 'father/mother,' 'teacher/builder/ landscape architect/writer,' 'an American' and so on. Titles and roles such as these are another way of trying to override our fragile sense of self. We feel that we *are* someone because of them.

Moral exclusion

One of the most dangerous aspects of group identity is what psychologists call 'moral exclusion.' This happens when we withdraw moral and human rights from other groups, and deny them respect and justice. Moral standards are only applied to members of our own group. We treat our own kind fairly, sharing resources with them and making sacrifices and supporting and encouraging their development. But this benevolence comes to an abrupt end once the group boundary is crossed, switching to hostility and callousness to outsiders. Because we have excluded them from our 'moral community,' it's all too easy for us to exploit, oppress and even kill them.

My view is that this behavior is related to our ego-separateness. As I suggested in the last chapter, 'man's inhumanity to man' is fuelled by a lack of empathy. Because we are 'walled-off' within our egos, what might be termed our 'circle of empathy' is very narrow. If we feel any degree of empathy at all, it's only to the people who are closest to us, who are most similar to us and share our identity.

This helps to explain the puzzle of why some people can be compassionate to their own family and community, and yet sadistically cruel to others outside their group. Even Hitler was known to be caring and considerate to his inner circle of staff. In a recent interview his maid, now in her 90s, recalled that, 'I only ever knew Hitler as a kindly man who was good to me.'[5] Similarly, his bodyguard recalled how Hitler would let his personal physician treat him if he felt ill, would give him time off to go on dates with girls, and how he treated him with gifts when he got married. (Famously, Hitler is thought to have been a vegetarian too, although it's not clear whether this was motivated by empathy for animals or for health reasons.)

Group identity and conflict

Once a group identity has developed, oppression and conflict are never far away. Most conflicts throughout history have been a clash between two or more different 'identity groups' – the Christians and Muslims in the Crusades, the Jews and Arabs, Hindus and Muslims in India, the Catholics and Protestants in Northern Ireland, the Israelis and Palestinians, the Serbs, Croats and Bosnians and so on.

The sense of group identity facilitates the collective pathology discussed in the last chapter. It allows one group to collectively feel a desire to conquer and subjugate other groups, in order to increase their wealth and power. In times of stability and wealth, different groups can coexist without conflict, even in relative harmony. But often it only takes a degree of hardship or upheaval for underlying tensions to erupt; or else external powers may purposely ignite that tension for their own benefit.

In India, Muslims and Hindus lived together largely peacefully until the late nineteenth century. Some historians argue that, until the beginning of that century, Hindus and Muslims in India didn't even have a distinct communal identity. The British colonists of India encouraged a sense of group identity by treating the groups differently, deliberately inflaming tensions between them with a 'divide and rule' policy[6]. As general animosity toward the British grew, the tensions between Hindus and Muslims intensified too, until they exploded into massive violence and bloodshed in the Partition of 1947. India became independent of the British, and the old country was split into India and Pakistan. More than 14 million people moved countries, Hindus from the new Pakistan moving south to the new India, and Muslims moving north to Pakistan (or east to present-day Bangladesh, at the time called East Pakistan). Almost inevitably – as Gandhi had predicted – displaced Hindu and Muslim groups turned on each other, and around 500,000 people died.

In Yugoslavia, different ethnic groups had lived together so peacefully that Bosnia and Sarajevo were once seen as examples of successfully integrated societies. But Yugoslavia was badly hit by the foreign debt crisis in the 1980s, resulting in tension between different groups. And following the dissolution of the Soviet Bloc, the economic situation grew much worse, as the other ex-communist states began to compete for Western trade. Poverty was greater than at any time since World War II and, as a result, people began to identify more with their ethnic groups and to demand independence.

This need for ethnic identity was increased by the 'identity vacuum' created by the dissolution of the Communist Bloc. People who had once identified themselves as communists and perceived capitalist countries as 'the other' now fell back on their old ethnic identities – Serbs, Bosnians, Croats, Albanians, and so on, or as Christians or Muslims. 'The other' was now other ethnic groups. The media and politicians demonized these groups too, at the same time as intensifying national pride and self-assertion. Consequently, in 1991 the old Republic of Yugoslavia broke up into warring factions, resulting in around 140,000 deaths.

As these examples show, group identity is a fluid process. Identity is never fixed; people can take it from different sources at different times. In times when there is no identity readily available, people will always *create* one. This explains the tendency for one group of people to split into smaller groups, who then fall into conflict with one another. Time and again, larger religious, political or cultural groups have divided into 'splinter groups' with a new, distinct identity of their own. This partly explains why there are so many different groups who refer to themselves as 'Christians': Catholics, Protestants, Anglicans, Baptists, Lutherans, Methodists, Jehovah's Witnesses, and so on. This was another source of bemusement for the Native Americans. As the Seneca Chief Red Jacket said to the European settlers: 'You say there is but one way to worship and serve the Great Spirit. If there is but one religion, why do you white people differ so much about it? Why not all agreed, as you can all read the Book?'[7]

Neo-Darwinists or evolutionary psychologists would no doubt explain all of this in genetic terms. They would argue that it's natural for people who are genetically related to group together, and for one group of genetically similar people to be in conflict with other groups. As they see it, our main interest as human beings is to protect and replicate our genes, so we're programmed to look after people close to us – in our genetically related group – but not people in other groups, who have a different genetic makeup. However, as the above examples show, people often form groups based on *ideology* rather than ethnic or racial differences. And even without ideology, it often happens that miniscule differences within groups – such as different professions or classes – slowly build up into clear dividing lines and lead to group conflict.

One of the most graphic and horrific examples of this was the genocide in Rwanda in 1994 that left around 750,000 people dead, about 20 percent of the country's whole population. This conflict didn't originate in any real tribal or ethnic division, but in artificial group identities created by the German and Belgian colonial powers. Originally, the Hutus and Tutsis weren't separate groups. Even today, they speak exactly the same language, live in the same areas and follow the same traditions. The term 'Tutsi' simply applied to a Rwandan who owned a lot of cattle, while 'Hutu' applied to the others who didn't. But a Tutsi could easily become a Hutu and vice versa. However, when the Germans colonized Rwanda in the 1890s they decided that the Tutsi looked more European and treated them preferentially. Later, when Belgians colonists took over from the Germans, they encouraged this division by giving Rwandans identity cards labeling them as 'Tutsi' or 'Hutu.' As a result, a clear dividing line was established between the two groups, a clear sense of 'otherness,' which allowed moral exclusion to take place. Animosity between the groups festered until it exploded into genocide after the President Habyarimana was assassinated in April 1994.

Groups are created by the psychological need for identity, not genetic similarities or differences – although, of course, this psychological need will often *make use of* preexisting ethnic or racial differences.

The madness of dogmatic religion

Our need to reinforce the ego through our identity and belonging goes some way toward explaining another type of human behavior that an indigenous anthropologist might find difficult to understand: dogmatic religion.

I've met many religious people who are compassionate and spiritual, whose religion serves as a framework for their moral and spiritual development. I also know that many of the rituals and practices of religion can have a powerful spiritual effect, bringing a sense of sacredness and inner peace. But at the same time, there are many religious people who are mad, and many religious beliefs and practices that can be seen as mad.

It's important to make a distinction between 'spiritual' and 'dogmatic' religion. Spiritual religion is the type I've described above. It promotes the higher attributes of human nature, like altruism and compassion, and fosters a sense of the sacred and sublime. Spiritually religious people don't feel any animosity to other religious groups – in fact, they're happy to investigate other beliefs, and may even go to other groups' temples and services. They aren't usually evangelical; their attitude is that different religions are suited to different people, and that all religions are different manifestations or expressions of the same essential truths.

Unfortunately spiritual religion is the less common form. Most of the world's religious people practice dogmatic religion. Dogmatically religious people think that they're right and everyone else is wrong. For them, religion isn't about self-development or experiencing the transcendent, but about adhering to a set of rigid beliefs and following the rules laid down by religious authorities. It's about defending their beliefs against anyone who questions them, asserting their 'truth' over the beliefs of others and spreading their beliefs to everyone else. For them, the fact that other people have different beliefs is an affront, since it implies the possibility that their own beliefs may be false. They need to convince other people that they're wrong to prove to themselves that they're right.

I'm aware that I'm polarizing the issue somewhat here – of course, there is a large gray area between these two types. It's certainly not always a question of either/or. Some people may hold firm religious beliefs at the same time as feeling an all-embracing altruism, a spiritual desire to serve others and relieve their suffering, irrespective of their faith. (Mother Theresa was a good example of this, a devout Catholic who devoted her life to serving the poorest Indian people.) They may be convinced that their religion is the most 'correct' version of the truth but at the same time fully respect the beliefs of others.

But speaking in terms of polarities, the purpose of dogmatic religion is to *strengthen* the ego, through beliefs, labels and group identity. However, the purpose of spiritual religion is the complete opposite of this – to *transcend* the ego, through compassion, altruism, and spiritual practice.

The origins of religion

Essentially, dogmatic religion can be seen as the result of several different aspects of ego-madness working together.

The madness of dogmatic religion begins with the amazing plasticity of the childhood psyche, which makes it possible for parents and other authorities to pass on religious belief-systems. As I mentioned earlier, if beliefs are 'implanted' in the structure of the psyche during its development in infancy, they become so deeply ingrained that they are very difficult to dislodge. No matter how bizarre they might seem to outsiders, to the person they are self-evident truths. Humanists sometimes imply that it's possible to use reason to defeat religious beliefs but it's by no means as simple as this. When beliefs are ingrained in the deep structure of a person's psyche, using rational argument to prove that they're wrong is as futile as trying to convince a person with schizophrenia to return to sanity.

The origins of religious beliefs

It's often assumed that belief in gods is natural to human beings, and that we have always believed in them, but this isn't strictly true. Most of the world's indigenous peoples didn't believe in gods, as we understand the term. Rather than the worship of gods, their religion – if we can use that word to describe it – is based on their sense that the whole world, and everything in it, is pervaded with an animating force. This isn't an all-powerful anthropomorphic entity like a god, but usually an impersonal, disembodied energy. Almost all indigenous groups have a different word for this force. In Africa, the Nuer call it *kwoth* and the Mbuti *pepo*. In America, the Pawnee call it *tirawa*, and the Lakota call it *wakan-tanka* (literally, the 'force which moves all things'). Elsewhere, the Ainu of Japan call it *ramut,* while in New Guinea it is *imunu* (translated as 'soul').

As well as sensing this all-pervading energy – or Spirit – in the world, most indigenous peoples see the world as populated with individual spirits. Again, it's a mistake to think of spirits as deities. They aren't thought of as having an anthropomorphic form, but in a more abstract way, as forces or powers, similar to shades or vapors. There are two types of spirits: the spirits of dead people and nature spirits which are connected to different natural phenomena and sometimes inhabit them. These nature spirits live inside stones, animals, rivers, and the wind, and have a function in explaining natural events. When a person gets ill, it's because a bad spirit has entered the body; when it starts raining it's because the spirit of the rain is aroused, and so on. (This is the one sense in which spirits are similar to gods. In theistic religion, gods take on this explanatory role. For example, if a person becomes ill and dies, it is 'God's will'; if it starts raining it's because the god of rain has 'woken up.')

In my view, the concept of God as anthropomorphic omnipotent entity who oversees the world and controls the events of our lives is another result of our humania – in particular, a reaction to the sense of ego-separateness and incompleteness. If you believe that God is always watching over you, then it means that you're never alone. 'He' provides a comforting sense of communion, which helps to alleviate our sense of isolation, of being trapped inside our mental space with the rest of reality 'out there.'

In addition, this concept of a personal god is a psychological response to fear. To a large extent, fear stems from the randomness of events. We fear the future because it's unknown and unpredictable, and potentially filled with dangers, like a dark forest. There is the fear of natural disasters, of illness, of death, of losing loved ones or your livelihood and so on. But if you believe that God is controlling events and if you're confident that their ultimate outcome will be positive, then there's no randomness and no (or at least less) fear. Everything is pre-ordained, part of a divine plan.

The concept of an afterlife is also an important part of the appeal of religions, of course. Indigenous peoples have beliefs in an afterlife too but they generally don't conceive of the afterlife as heaven or a paradise, where their every need will be met and they'll exist in a state of bliss for all eternity. Many peoples believe that in the next world they'll just go on living in much the same way as in this life, only as a shade or spirit. Others have a more spiritual conception of death, seeing it as a time when our individual spirit merges back into Spirit as a whole, or when we return to the womb of the Earth.[8]

However, because humania means that our lives are so full of suffering – both psychological suffering and the social suffering of oppression and conflict – for us the afterlife became an idyllic place that could compensate us for the privations of life on Earth. It became a kind of collective pipedream that helped us to endure the misery of the present, a future place where we would gain everything that eluded us in this life: contentment, fulfillment, gratification of all our desires. Particularly for our ancestors – whose lives were 'nasty, brutish, and short' as peasants, serfs or slaves – to believe in an idyllic afterlife was a psychological necessity, without which life would have seemed a cruel and meaningless joke.

Group identity and power

Religion can help satisfy a whole spectrum of human needs, from the highest to the lowest. You can think of this in terms of Abraham Maslow's 'hierarchy of needs.' In its spiritual form, religion can help satisfy the need for 'self-actualization' – the highest human need, according to Maslow. It can help us to develop morality and compassion, to transcend self-centeredness and separateness, and to develop a sense of the sacred. And lower on the hierarchy, in its dogmatic form, religion can help satisfy our basic needs for security and identity.

Once religious beliefs are formed, they provide a basis for group identity. A religious group establishes itself, and – as well as being passed on to the children of members of the group – other people take on its beliefs, because they need the sense of identity and belonging that the group provides. Aside from ethnic identity, dogmatic religion is probably human beings' biggest source of group identity, and group conflict. And often, of course, ethnic and religious identities are tied together, as in the cases of Irish Protestants and Irish Catholics, and Bosnian Muslims and Serbian Christians. One reinforces the other, and makes the potential for conflict even greater.

Often the need for status and power uses dogmatic religion as a vehicle too. In addition to being a way of dealing with the affront of different beliefs, the urge to convert others to your religion stems from a desire to extend power. Ultimately, dogmatically religious people want the same outcome as the imperialists or colonists: to conquer the whole world with their beliefs. Dogmatically religious people speak fondly of 'spreading the Good News,' but really they're acting out of the same impulse for power and control that drove Alexander the Great or Stalin. When the Communist Bloc dissolved at the end of the 1980s, there was a massive influx of religious missionaries to the former Communist countries – Mormons, Jehovah's Witnesses, born-again Christians and others. At the same time, there was a massive influx of Western companies, eager to open up the new markets. And essentially, both the missionaries and the business executives wanted the same thing: to extend their empires.

One of the reasons why humanists are so opposed to religion is that they believe it is divisive and creates conflict. There's no doubt that this is true. But to paraphrase my earlier point about conflict and genetic differences, it's not religion that creates division and conflict, but the psychological need for group identity. If religion wasn't available as a way of providing group identity, people would – and do, of course – find other sources of identity: ethnic or regional differences, political beliefs or football teams.

This is part of the reason why, despite the endeavors of dogmatic atheists such as Richard Dawkins, who believe that it will eventually be superseded by science and reason, dogmatic religion will never disappear. For many of us in the Western world, life is relatively free of hardship and oppression, and so religion isn't *as* important to us as it was to our ancestors. There isn't as much suffering in our lives, so we don't have such a strong need for the pipedream of an idyllic afterlife. However, there's still *some need* for religion, of course, because our psychological suffering is still there. We all need some way of dealing with the psychological suffering caused by humania. Some of us try to alleviate it by losing ourselves in distractions and activities; some of us try to deal with it by chasing after wealth and status; others use quasi-religious activities, like following a football team or a political party. In fact, because rationalism and science have made religion less credible, these methods have become more and more popular. But dogmatic religion itself is still an effective response to humania and will always be used by some people. Dogmatic religion will persist as long as humania does.

CHAPTER 8
The Origins of Humania

Unlike physical illnesses, it's very difficult to identify the causes of mental disorders. For example, no one is really sure what causes schizophrenia. Many different possibilities have been suggested e.g. genetic factors, brain chemistry (for example, an imbalance between dopamine and serotonin), a head injury, or even a viral infection, together with environmental factors such as trauma or drug abuse.

But what about humania? I've said that the condition consists of two basic characteristics: the separateness of the ego and our cognitive discord. Is it possible to say why we developed these characteristics?

Perhaps the best way to start is by looking at people who *don't* suffer from the condition.

The harmony of indigenous peoples

I've already suggested that many of the world's indigenous peoples don't seem to suffer from humania, at least to nowhere near the same extent that we do. And if that's true, what makes them different to us?

I've mainly been referring to Native American groups, but there are, of course, countless other indigenous groups, including the different Australian Aboriginal groups, the tribal groups of the forests and hills of India, of Borneo, New Guinea, Polynesia, and so on. Tragically, a large number of these cultures have been destroyed or disrupted by contact with Europeans, and as a result many groups now suffer from severe social and psychological problems. However, there are some communities – particularly in very isolated areas – who still live a traditional way of life.

It was because these peoples showed so few signs of humania that European colonists and missionaries found them so hard to understand, and saw them as inferior and even subhuman. For example, early colonists were shocked at how 'lazy' indigenous peoples seemed to be, because they didn't seem to share the European need to escape from their own psyche through activity and distraction. For Europeans, idleness was a sin that could even leave you vulnerable to the devil's influence, as in the saying 'the devil will find work for idle hands to do.' But in America, the Indians would only work for as long as necessary. They would sometimes work for six months and then rest for the following six. They felt no need to carry on working to accumulate a surplus of food or other goods to store or sell.

Similarly, when anthropologists began close observation of traditional hunter–gatherer peoples, they were shocked to find that they spent very little time 'working.' They found that they only spent between 12 and 20 hours a week searching for food.[1] The rest of their time was theirs to fill as they wanted. Even nowadays, traditional Aboriginal Australians only spend around four hours a day searching for food. They spend the rest of their time singing, storytelling, making art, and chatting with family and friends.[2] In other words, 'doing nothing' didn't seem to be a problem for them. Many modern indigenous peoples still seem to have an enviable ability to sit quietly, doing nothing in particular, without feeling any restlessness or frustration.

This is why many of these peoples seem to have an amazing ability to *wait*. Anthropologists have noted that although indigenous peoples might have to wait hours for the weather to change so that they can go hunting or for the sea to calm down so they can go fishing, or even days for a mountain pass to clear of snow, they rarely seem to show any sign of urgency or impatience. Several years ago, for example, the anthropologists Andrew Miracle and Juan de Dios noted that the Aymara Indians of Chile showed no signs of agitation whatsoever, even if they had to wait hours for a truck to take them to market.[3] The American anthropologist Edward T. Hall observed that the Native Americans he lived with never showed any frustration when waiting for hours at hospitals or trading posts, whereas Europeans would become bad-tempered and restless.[4] It's our need to latch our attention to activities or entertainments that makes waiting so frustrating for us. When we wait, we don't have any choice except to do nothing. We don't have anywhere to focus our attention – except perhaps to a few old magazines or dreary daytime TV shows – and so we have to turn inside ourselves and experience our psychological discord.

In other words, it may be that indigenous peoples don't experience the same degree of psychological discord as us. They seem to possess a more unified and peaceful kind of psyche. This fits with the reports of anthropologists too, who have consistently described them as possessing a striking *joie de vivre,* a carefree and cheerful attitude, even in the face of difficulties. This was certainly one of the characteristics that struck early colonists and explorers. For example, the early eighteenth-century explorer Kolben described the South African Hottentots as 'the most friendly, the most liberal and the most benevolent people to one another that ever appeared on the Earth.' After quoting this remark in his 1902 book *Mutual Aid: a Factor of Evolution*, the Russian zoologist and philosopher Peter Kropotkin noted that similar words have 'continually appeared since in the description of savages... the Ostyaks, the Samoyedes, the Eskimos, the Dayaks, the Aleoutes, the Papaus, and so on, by the highest authorities. I also remember having read them applied to the Tunguses, the Tchuktchis, the Sioux, and several others.'[5]

In modern times, the English anthropologist Colin Turnbull described the life of the pygmies of central Africa – who he lived with for three years in the 1950s – as 'a wonderful thing, full of joy and happiness and free of care.'[6] While more recently still, the anthropologist Daniel Everett has written in similar terms of the Piraha Indians of the Amazon: 'Since my first night among them I have been impressed with their patience, their happiness and their kindness.' He goes on to say that the Piraha 'show no evidence of depression, chronic fatigue, extreme anxiety, panic attacks, or other psychological ailments common in many industrialized societies.'[7]

Of course, happiness is a very subjective state, and the impressions of explorers or anthropologists can't be taken as real evidence. And even if it's true that these peoples experience greater wellbeing than us, other factors could be involved, such as closeness to nature, a lower level of stress, and a more cohesive community. But this is certainly the kind of wellbeing we would expect from individuals who don't suffer from humania. Mihaly Csikszentmihalyi also suggests that indigenous peoples appear to be free of what he calls 'psychic entropy,' noting that they 'often display a serenity that seems enviable to the visitor from more differentiated cultures.'[8] And it's worth noting that no indigenous peoples have ever commented on the apparent serenity and benevolence of European colonists – in fact, as we have seen, all of their comments were to the contrary.

I've already suggested that indigenous peoples generally lack the impulse to collect material goods, and also that they are very egalitarian, with a similar indifference to status and power. The latter is particularly true of hunter–gatherer groups. The anthropologist James Woodburn speaks of the 'profound egalitarianism' of the 'immediate return' hunter–gatherer groups (meaning groups that live by immediately using any good or resources they collect). He remarks that 'no other way of human life permits so great an emphasis on equality.'[9] He describes them as follows:

> ...societies of equals – equals in wealth, equals in power, and equals in status... In these societies equality is actively promoted and inequality is actively resisted through a set of coherent interlocked and mutually reinforcing institutional procedures.[10]

In these groups, nobody has the right to tell anybody else what to do, and group decisions are made democratically. Even if there is a chief (in some cases there isn't) their power is limited, and he or she can't take any action against the will of the majority. Another anthropologist, Christopher Boehm, has remarked that the modern day United Nations works in a strikingly similar way to hunter–gatherer groups, with its member states reaching collective decisions by consensus[11].

Women usually have high status in indigenous groups too. In pre-colonial Africa, for instance, women were often chiefs and village leaders, and councils often had female members. Native American women had a large degree of authority too: they often had the job of nominating new chiefs, for example, and when agreements were made between Indian groups and early Europeans, documents had to be signed by women, since the marks of men carried no authority. Similarly, in Tahiti, women could become chiefs, were free to play sports with men, and had a great deal of sexual freedom. In 'immediate return' hunter–gatherer groups, men usually have no authority over women at all. Women usually choose their marriage partners, decide what work they want to do, and work whenever they choose. If a marriage breaks down they have custody rights over their children.[12] The high status of women in these societies – together with their open attitude toward sex – makes the idea that a woman can be killed for having sex before marriage or asking for a divorce appear even more insane.

Indigenous peoples were also generally peaceful and un-warlike. This is a controversial topic, because we've been conditioned into thinking of these peoples as primitive 'savages,' who went around bashing each other over the head with clubs and throwing spears at strangers. Many of us have also grown up watching cowboy movies full of images of savage Indians fighting ferociously and scalping the heads of anyone they captured. There are also evolutionary psychologists (such as Steven Pinker) who believe that war is fundamental to human nature, and try to show – usually by manipulating or cherry-picking the evidence – that it was just as common in prehistoric and indigenous societies as in more recent ones[13]. However, many anthropologists accept that, in their natural environment, indigenous peoples are extremely peaceful, and go to great lengths to avoid conflict. They rarely, if ever, show any desire to 'conquer' other tribal groups and take hold of their wealth and territory. In his book *The Origin of War*, for example, the anthropologist J.M.G. van der Dennen surveys more than 500 tribal groups, the vast majority of whom he finds to be 'highly un-warlike' with a small proportion who have 'mild, low-level, and/or ritualized warfare.'[14]

The different tribes of the Australian Aborigines, for example, very rarely fought against each other. Even when they did it was common to 'ritualize' the conflict into a fight between two individuals. A representative of each tribe would be chosen, and the two men would stand motionless, about 15 to 20 meters apart, and throw spears at each other. When one of them was wounded the 'war' would be over[15]. One potential source of conflict among Aborigines is when hunters from one tribe approach the campsite of another tribe. But here there is another traditional ritual that defuses the situation. The hunters wait at a distance from the campsite, making sure they can be seen. Then the unmarried members of the hunting group, and those who have been apart from their wives for a long time, lie down on their backs. At sunset a group of women from the tribe walk over from the campsite, lie down on top of the hunters, and have sex with them[16].

It may be that indigenous peoples are largely free of these pathological traits because they are largely free of ego-isolation and cognitive discord. They obviously experience themselves as individuals to a degree, but – as I pointed out at the beginning of Chapter 2 – their sense of individuality is less sharp than ours. Their sense of ego isn't so strong that it creates a sense of separateness between them and other people, other creatures, their land, and the Earth itself. As a result, they don't suffer from the sense of separateness and lack that has so many negative consequences in our lives.

Their ability to wait and do nothing and their intense perception suggests that indigenous peoples' minds aren't as disturbed by thought-chatter as ours either. When Jung asked the Native American Chief in New Mexico why he thought Europeans were mad, he replied as follows:

> *'They say they think with their heads.'*
> *'Why, of course,' said Jung, 'What do you think with?'*
> *'We think here,' said Chief Mountain Lake, indicating his heart.*[17]

As a result, indigenous peoples' mental space may well be more harmonious than ours, so that they're quite content to rest within it. If we're like teenagers who can't stay in their parents' house because the atmosphere is full of acrimony, then indigenous peoples are more akin to the children of a happily married couple, whose house is peaceful and comfortable.

The fall

The question is why did *we* develop humania, while these peoples apparently didn't, at least not to anything like the same degree?

It's impossible to give a conclusive answer to this question, but one possibility is that ego-madness was a psychological change that occurred at some point in our ancestors' history. Fundamentally, humania is caused by a very strong ego-structure, with powerful boundaries – the 'over-developed ego,' as I sometimes call it. There's some evidence that this strong sense of ego may have developed around 6,000 years ago, over several centuries during the fourth millennium BCE.

The ancestors of most modern Europeans, Middle Eastern, and Asian peoples – the peoples who suffer from humania most severely – stemmed from central Asia and the Middle East. Archeological records show that they began migrating away from their homelands during the fourth millennium BCE. From around this time, signs of a new individuality started appearing: individual rather than communal burials, personal property, texts that describe the names and deeds of individuals, and myths showing a shift from the impersonal to the personal. There was a massive eruption of warfare throughout central Asia and the Middle East, together with the first signs of patriarchal and hierarchical societies.

If it's possible to locate the psychological change at any point in history, this may be it. And it is just possible – although I stress that this is just a speculative hypothesis – that the psychological change may be linked to an environmental change. Until 4000BCE, central Asia and the Middle East had been fertile and full of animal and plant life, but around this time a process of severe and widespread desertification took hold. Rainfall decreased, rivers and lakes evaporated, vegetation disappeared and famine took hold.

Farming became impossible and lack of water made hunting treacherous. The areas were intensely populated (at least compared to other parts of the world at this time) but now there was a mass exodus of animals and people from the region, as groups migrated in search of more fertile areas.

This environmental change may have caused a psychological shift in our ancestors, encouraging the growth of a new sharpened and more separate ego. On the one hand, it may have promoted a new kind of selfishness and individuality. People were forced to think in terms of their individual survival rather than in terms of their community's. At the same time, these difficulties may have promoted a new kind of intelligence. It's possible that in order to survive, people had to develop better problem-solving skills, great powers of logic and abstract thought, as well as a new ability to plan for the future. And this kind of intelligence demands a stronger sense of ego, because the ego is the part of our minds we think *with*. The ego gives us powers of self-reflection and abstraction, together with the ability to imagine the future. Indigenous peoples had – and have – these abilities to a degree, of course, but they became much more developed in our ancestors.

In itself, this type of intelligence was, of course, a very positive development. These cognitive abilities have made it possible for us to build cities, fly to the moon, invent computers, develop life-saving medical procedures and so on. But the massive dark side to these cognitive developments was the separateness and discord of the ego.

If this is true, then the probable reason why indigenous peoples don't suffer from humania is because they didn't experience this psychological shift. Perhaps this is simply because they didn't undergo the same massive environmental change as our ancestors, and so never developed a strong ego-structure. As a result, they never suffered from the massive psychological and social problems that humania generates.

Colonial madness

The massive problem they *did* encounter, however, was their encounter with European colonists who were afflicted with humania. The conquest, decimation, and cultural destruction of indigenous tribes by Europeans is a chilling example of the destructive power of ego-madness.

When a group of 'humaniacs' encounters a group who don't suffer from the condition, they will inevitably destroy them. The former's desire for power and wealth, together with their lack of empathy, will drive them to subjugate and eventually eliminate the other group – especially since, with no traditions of social oppression and warfare, the latter are unlikely to have the temperament or the weapons to resist the brutality and military might of their opponents.

And this is exactly what has happened to the world's indigenous peoples. Contact with Europeans was toxic to them, as deadly as the bubonic plague, and their populations declined with shocking rapidity. It's impossible to say exactly what the population of the American continent was before Columbus' arrival, but estimates range from 20 to 100 million. However, by 1920 the indigenous population of the USA and Canada had shrunk to just 220,000. In Australia, the Aboriginal population declined shockingly from at least 1 million before European invasion to only 30,000 by the 1930s.[18]

Just 500 years ago indigenous groups occupied most of the Earth's surface, including the whole of the American continent and Australia. Now the groups are almost invisible, while 'humaniacs' dominate the world, culturally and geographically. The end point of humania is complete domination, the conquest of the whole planet – although unfortunately this also equates with our own destruction as a species.

The loss of childhood harmony

However, we don't have to travel the world in search of people who are free of humania. There may even be some of them in your house; at the very least you'll walk past them on the street every day.

I'm talking about children, of course. Like indigenous peoples, children don't experience themselves as an 'I' inside their heads, as a fragile ego separated from a world 'out there.' They don't feel as if they're apart from the world but are immersed in it, like people swimming in the river, rather than people on the bank watching it flow. As a result, children aren't plagued by feelings of aloneness and incompleteness. They don't feel a sense of lack, and a need to bolster their identity.

In addition, children's minds don't seem to continually buzz away with thoughts about the future and the past, replaying and anticipating scenes from their lives. They seem to be free of the kind of negative thoughts that afflict us as adults and the feelings of worry, anxiety, bitterness or regret that those thoughts trigger. When was the last time you heard a five-year-old girl say, 'I'm a bit worried about this birthday party I've got to go to next week. I don't know the other children very well so I'm scared that I might be left out'? When was the last time you heard a five-year-old boy say, 'That boy over there ignored me when I walked past him last week, so I'm not talking to him today.' Children give themselves wholly to the present. Pascal's complaint that we spend our lives 'wandering in times which do not belong to us' certainly doesn't apply to them. They spend very little time in a state of 'elsewhereness.'

This is one of the reasons why, when people look back at their childhood, they often remark on how real and intense everything seemed then, how colors seemed brighter and flavors and tastes seemed richer. This is partly because the world is so new and fresh to children, as they haven't yet become desensitized to their experience. But it's also a simple matter of *attention*. Whatever they do – whether it's eating some chocolate, having a bath, listening to a song or a nursery rhyme or playing on the swings – children pay *full attention* to their experience. There is no thought-chatter to take their attention away from the is-ness of their perceptions and sensations. In a play area, they don't waste time thinking about what they're going to do at nursery tomorrow, or compare this play area to others they've been to recently – they give themselves completely to the joy and excitement of playing. Even when we adults don't think distinctly about a particular subject, there is still usually a vague mental fog inside our heads, made up of undefined images and scraps of concepts and ideas, which dilutes the intensity of our perceptions and sensations. Without this fog of abstraction, children's experience is richer and fresher.

In other words, young children experience much less psychological discord than adults. (They certainly experience *emotional* discord frequently, usually displayed as intense waves of anger or frustration when their desires aren't met or when they feel tired and insecure. But these pass through them very quickly and don't leave any traces of discontent behind.) As a result, they aren't as vulnerable to anxiety when they have unstructured free time or when there's quietness and stillness around them. Of course, children like to be active and creative, and will eagerly watch TV if their parents let them, but – apart from perhaps a brief storm of frustration – they don't feel a sense of unease when activities come to an end. One of the differences between them and adults is that children latch their attention to external 'hooks' *solely* because the activity or the entertainment is interesting to them, whereas we often do this as a way of escaping from the discord inside us.

This is also why children don't need to take drugs or drink alcohol, why they don't need material goods, and why they don't need to define themselves in terms of their ethnic group or religion (although that doesn't stop adults foisting religion on them, of course). There's no discontent for them to try to override, no incompleteness for them to fill, no sense of insignificance to compensate for. My children go to an inner-city school where there is a vibrant mixture of ethnic groups and religions. The school is roughly made up of one-third white kids, a third black and a third Asian. At the time of writing, my older kids are eight and five, and it's truly wonderful how they and their classmates don't differentiate at all between different social identities. They relate to each other purely as other human beings, independent of all concepts. As a result, they mix together perfectly. (My eldest son's two best friends are both Asian boys.) This intermingling is common among young children, but usually by the time they reach 11 to 12, they begin to assume ethnic and religious differences, resulting in more differentiation.

This lack of ego-madness in infants is simply a question of psychological development. Since our ancestors developed it thousands of years ago, the strong ego-structure has been part of the 'blueprint' of our psychological development. Young children are free of it simply because they haven't reached that stage of development yet. Psychologists believe that young babies don't have any sense of self whatsoever, and have no sense of separation between themselves and the world. The sense of self – and of separation – appears to develop from the age of six months, but only becomes fully developed in the late teens, at roughly the same stage that we become fully developed physically. Young children – say, before the age of eight or nine – have a very flimsy sense of self. The boundary between their self-structure and the world is very weak, like a fragile wire-mesh fence between two fields. The 'ego-boundary' only solidifies around the mid-teens, when we first begin to have a clear sense of inhabiting our bodies, of being a 'ghost in the machine.'

The origins of thought-chatter

A similar process occurs with thought-chatter. You can see thought-chatter as a by-product of our strong ego-structure, which develops in parallel with it, beginning to take over our minds during our mid-to-late-teens. At a certain point, we develop the ability to talk to ourselves inside our heads, to hold an inner dialogue with ourselves, to deliberate and interpret our experience. This may have happened historically, at the point when our ancestors developed a strong ego-structure and more acute cognitive powers, and it happens to us all in our own psychological development, as we move toward adolescence.

This self-reflection should be – and often is – very beneficial to us. These are the 'powers of reason' which supposedly make us superior to animals, able to organize our lives, to evaluate situations, make plans and decisions and so on. But unfortunately this self-reflective ability seems to have malfunctioned. Like a computer that has developed a will of its own, the mechanism has slipped out of our control and produces an endless chaotic series of impressions and images.

Thought-chatter is the result of the interaction of this self-reflective ability combined with our faculties of memory, imagination and anticipation. When self-reflection becomes automatic and random, it interacts with the faculty of memory and replays scenes from our past; it interacts with the faculty of imagination and creates imaginary realities for us to inhabit; it interacts with the faculty of anticipation – the ability to plan and envisage the future – and allows us to create scenarios of future events. It should really be seen as a psychological aberration, a kind of quirk of the mind.

The difficulties of adolescence

It's the development of the strong ego that makes adolescence such a difficult period for some people. The freshness and joy of childhood gives way to dullness and confusion. After being part of the flow of experience in the world, we're suddenly *outside* the world, alone inside our mental space. We lose the intense perception of our infancy, and begin to perceive the world through a mental fog, and to taste the discord and suffering of humania. And because humania is so new to us – and because it comes so quickly after the free and easy exuberance of childhood – we feel it especially intensely.

I remember this transition clearly from my adolescence. After a carefree childhood, I suddenly felt locked inside myself, alone with thoughts and feelings that no one else would ever be able to experience. Along with that, I felt an acute self-consciousness. I was conscious of every movement I made and every word I spoke, so that I couldn't do anything naturally anymore. I felt exposed when I walked down the street, aware that people could be looking at me from their windows. I only felt comfortable when I was locked in my bedroom at night. I didn't like the summer because the days were so long and bright, and so I felt more exposed and awkward.

The new adolescent ego is especially fragile and naked, which is why – as mentioned in the last chapter – adolescents have such a strong need for belonging, to be a part of groups and gangs, and why they are so sensitive to slights. This is probably the main strategy that adolescents use to deal with the fragility of the ego. However, as we become adults we start to use another strategy, which eventually becomes even more important to us. This is collecting attachments for the ego, adding things to it in order to make it stronger. In early adulthood, we take on the roles and labels of our jobs, of being husbands or wives or parents. We become psychologically attached to our beliefs, achievements and our knowledge, to hopes and ambitions, to our wealth and success, and so on. All of these things bolster the ego, like sandbags reinforcing a fragile sea wall. Eventually the ego becomes so strengthened by these attachments that the fragile adolescent ego is completely buried and obscured. We feel sturdier and more stable, but at the same time there's often a sense that something has been lost, that spontaneity and freshness have evaporated, and that the sheer weight of our attachments has walled us off from the world even further.

The fact that they didn't – and don't – suffer from humania doesn't make indigenous peoples or children superior to us. It doesn't mean that they represent an ideal state that we should aim to return to. I've already suggested that the development of the strong ego-structure gave us major cognitive benefits, and it would be foolish to sacrifice these. We need to go forward, not back, to a new state that retains those benefits – a new harmonious state in which we're free of the terrible suffering caused by humania. This will be a return to harmony and sanity – but a return to it in a *different* form.

And in the rest of this book we're going to examine how we can reach this state.

PART II
THE RETURN TO HARMONY AND SANITY

CHAPTER 9

Experiences of Harmony of Being

Several years ago I was unhappy at the college where I was teaching. A new manager had taken a dislike to me, and was going out of her way to make things difficult. One Friday afternoon I was taking our baby for a walk, mulling over my difficulties and feeling anxious about the prospect of going back to the college on Monday. All of a sudden, for no particular reason, my thoughts stopped. The mental fog dissipated, and my mind was completely empty and clear. I realized that there was no reason to worry. The situation at work was what it was; thinking about it wasn't going to change anything. In any case, it only existed in the future, in three days' time; it had nothing to do with me now.

This state of having a clear and empty mind seemed completely natural and right. The internal elsewhereness I'd been experiencing a few seconds ago – and which I'd slipped into most of the time since the problems began – seemed like a trance. It seemed absurd that I'd become so immersed in this state that I'd started to think of it as normal. Now I could feel a spaciousness and lightness inside me. And outside, the world looked beautiful. The trees and bushes were bright green and glistening with rain and every leaf seemed individual and distinct. The trees seemed alive, almost sentient. I suddenly started laughing aloud and knelt down to kiss baby Hugh.

This is a typical experience of what I call 'Harmony of Being.' These are experiences when we become temporarily free of humania, when our minds become quiet and still, free of cognitive discord, and we lose our normal sense of separateness and incompleteness.

Sometimes these experiences of harmony seem to come out of nowhere, for no apparent reason, as described above. You might experience it for a brief moment when you wake up in the morning after a good night's sleep. Just for a few seconds, before your thoughts start chattering away about the day ahead, your mind is empty and still, and you're filled with a strange sense of wellbeing and wholeness. Or another morning, when you wake up early, go downstairs and sit at the breakfast table – there's quietness and stillness around you, and you feel quiet and still inside too, with a glow of contentment spreading through you. You look through the window at the garden outside, just beginning to reveal itself in the dim light, and you're suddenly struck by its beauty. You feel as if you're seeing it in a different way to normal, seeing flowers and plants that you don't normally notice, and the whole landscape seems so still and yet at the same time so wild and alive.

Or you might experience harmony of being when you're watching your children play in the park in summer. You look around you, at the sunlight splashing through the trees and the perfect blue sky above you, and listen to your children's laughter – and the scene is so perfect that time seems to stand still. Or even when you're driving and are suddenly struck by the beauty of the evening sun, shining between the clouds and across the fields – just for a few moments, you feel lit up inside too, and a warm glow of wellbeing flows through your whole being.

Experiences of 'harmony of being'

Spontaneous experiences of harmony like these are quite rare though. Usually harmony of being is linked to certain activities or situations. For example, there are some sports that often give rise to the state. Several joggers and long-distance runners have told me that running has a powerful psychological effect on them, making them feel very calm and alert, and more 'grounded.' One colleague told me that he goes running every day because:

> It helps clear my mind, helps me get back to myself. It puts me back in tune with the world again, after all the hassles of work. All the work stuff fades from my mind and I just take pleasure from where I am, from the elements around me.

Swimming can also give rise to harmony. Once, when I was talking to a group of students about meditation, a young woman said to me, 'That's what I do when I go swimming!' She went on to say:

> When I'm swimming, I get into the rhythm of my movements and the gliding feeling of going through the water – I get so into it that I forget everything. I just feel the water against my skin and look up at the light shining on the water and the waves moving across the pool and it all looks perfect. When I get out of the water and get changed I feel happy and peaceful.

More dangerous and demanding pursuits can generate harmony too, such as climbing, flying or diving. Activities like these require so much concentration that they help us to forget the niggling concerns of daily life. The demands of the present – to make the next maneuver or avoid a potential danger – focus the mind so much that thought-chatter fades away and the future and the past cease to exist. As a result, climbers or pilots sometimes experience a sense of wholeness and contentment, becoming intensely aware of the beauty of their surroundings, and even feeling a sense of oneness with them.

The pilot Diane Ackerman, for instance – a 'compulsively pensive person,' as she describes herself – has said that she goes flying because it makes her feel 'fully alert but free of thought [which] is a form of ecstasy.'[1] Similarly, the American explorer Richard Byrd describes an experience of harmony he experienced during his second expedition to Antarctica, when he was alone in temperatures as low as -80C:

> *This was a grand period; I was conscious only of a mind utterly at peace, a mind adrift upon the smooth, romantic tides of imagination, like a ship responding to the strength and purpose in the enveloping medium. A man's moments of serenity are few, but a few will sustain him a lifetime. I found my measure of inward peace then; the stately echoes lasted a long time.*[2]

This is undoubtedly part of the reason why activities like these are so appealing. You might go running or swimming mainly because you want to keep fit; you might go climbing or flying mainly because you enjoy the sense of accomplishment at the end. But you're probably also attracted to these pursuits because of the inner harmony they generate, because they slow down your thought-chatter and clear your mind, making you feel alive and connected again. People who enjoy dangerous sports like paragliding, hang gliding or bungee jumping are sometimes called 'adrenaline junkies,' but it might be more accurate to describe them as 'harmony-seekers.' They may be seeking thrills, but they're also seeking harmony of being. The more demanding – and even dangerous – an activity, the more concentration it demands, and so the more it quiets the mind, and the more likely we are to enter into a state of harmony of being.

Sex often gives rise to harmony too, for similar reasons. The sensations we experience during sex are usually so pleasurable and powerful that they have a mind-quieting effect; thoughts about the past and future fade away, as we become completely present. Afterward, you're filled with a soothing glow of wellbeing, lying there with your partner in your arms, listening to the sounds of the night and staring into the warm, rich darkness. And then you might pull back the curtains and look at the scene outside your window, and feel that everything is somehow different. The clouds gliding across the sky seem somehow more real, as if an extra dimension has been added to them, and the black spaces between them seem somehow richer and thicker than before. And on the streets everything seems to be in its right place, the parked cars in front of your house and the trees and the streetlights along the side. The light of the lamps seems radiant and somehow benevolent.

Chemical changes are obviously significant here too. Part of the reason we feel euphoric after sex is because of the release of endorphins. This applies to running too, since endorphins are also released when we do strenuous exercise. But these experiences of harmony can't be wholly explained in chemical terms. They're mainly the result of a major psychological change that goes beyond physiology, in which cognitive discord decreases and ego-separation fades away.

Contact with nature is also a major source of harmony, and one of the main reasons why so many of us love being in the countryside. The beauty and grandeur of nature draws our attention away from thought-chatter, and the stillness and space relax us even further. As a result, our minds become quiet, and our ego-boundaries become softer, so that we transcend separateness and feel connected to our surroundings.

It's not surprising that recent research has found that contact with nature can be as effective against depression as therapy or medication. Researchers at the University of Essex in 2007 found that, of a group of people suffering from depression, 90 percent felt a higher level of self-esteem after a walk through a country park, and almost three-quarters felt less depressed. Another survey by the same research team found that 94 percent of people with mental illnesses believed that contact with nature put them in a more positive mood. Research such as this has led to the development of 'ecotherapy' – the use of contact with nature as a therapy by mental health professionals.[3]

Not only beautiful natural scenes, but any beautiful objects or phenomena can have a similar mind-quieting effect – a natural wonder, a great building, a great painting or piece of music. A visit to the Niagara Falls or the Taj Mahal, the amazing vividness of paintings like Van Gogh's

'Sunflowers' or Monet's 'Water Lilies' *(Nymphéas),* or the intoxicating melodies of the Beatles, Brian Wilson, Mozart or Mahler – all of these can stop the mind in its tracks and bring us fully into the present, into a state of harmony. And again, this is part of the reason why we feel so attracted to these beautiful scenes, objects, and sounds – not just because of their aesthetic quality, but also because of the psychological effect they have on us. We go out of our way to experience them because they have the power to halt the background hum of our thought-chatter for a while, to temporarily empty our minds and release us from anxiety and discord.

This is part of the appeal of vacations too. People go away for different reasons, of course: to relax and recharge our batteries, to drink and have fun, meet new romantic partners, to take ourselves away from the chores and problems of our daily lives. But perhaps the main reason why vacations are so important to us – strange though it might sound at first – is that they can bring us closer to inner harmony, by heightening our awareness and slowing down our minds.

One of the reasons why we generally don't pay attention to our everyday surroundings is simply because they're so familiar to us. We're so used to them that we've 'switched off' to their is-ness. They're only half-real to us, and so they don't seem deserving of our attention, in the same way that a repeat of a dreary old TV show doesn't seem worth watching. But when you visit new places – assuming you go to an unfamiliar environment rather than just a tourist complex – you're exposed to unfamiliarity. The foreign buildings and streets and the different food, language, and culture are more real to you. They're so new and different that you don't switch off from them. You pay them much more attention, and so are drawn out of internal elsewhereness, becoming much more present than you are at home. If it were somehow possible to measure how much thought-chatter runs through our minds, we would probably find that there's a lot less when we're away in unfamiliar environments. As a result, there's less cognitive discord inside us, and so we're closer to a state of harmony.

It's also important that we allow ourselves to relax on vacations. Normally we feel an internal pressure to keep busy, as if there's a kind of bullying manager inside us, saying, 'Come on, there's no time to relax, you've got to keep doing.' To some extent, in addition to being a response to our psychological discord, our busyness is a habit. Our constant activity builds up a momentum that is difficult to stop. But when we're away from our everyday environment, we allow this momentum to fade away, and the bullying manager falls silent. (Of course, the fact that there is less cognitive discord inside us makes it easier for us to do this.)

Absorption and focused attention

Whereas activities like reading and watching TV are a means of escape, the kinds of activities I've described above take us *closer* to reality. They take us *into* – rather than out of – ourselves and into the present.

One of the important distinctions here is that, whereas activities like reading and watching TV induce a state of absorption, activities like sport, appreciating art and contact with nature involve a *focusing* of the mind. Absorption and focused attention are different states, even though the difference between them is quite subtle. In absorption, your attention is so immersed in a particular task or distraction that you're 'sealed off' from the rest of your environment. You're enclosed in a circle of awareness. You might be dimly aware of other things happening on the periphery of that circle, and it may be easy for a new stimulus to break into it – for example, when you're working at the computer in your office and the phone rings or someone calls your name. You may also be partly internally elsewhere, and aware of the thoughts running through your mind. But essentially, you're out of the present and out of the real world, with your mind sealed off inside a 'pocket' of absorption. This is what happens in elsewhereness.

But in activities like swimming, sex, mountain climbing or flying we don't become wholly absorbed in this way. A mountain climber or a person staring at a great painting isn't, strictly speaking, *absorbed* in what they're doing – rather, they're in a state of focused attention. The difference is that although their attention is focused, it's not *immersed*. Even though it's narrowed to one area, it's not sealed off. As a result, they still have an open receptivity to the present. They don't close themselves off from the present, or from the rest of their environment, but remain part of it.

Flow

These states are very similar to the state that Csikszentmihalyi calls 'flow.' As he describes it, flow is a state in which we lose awareness of ourselves and our surroundings, and in which everything we do becomes effortless, every action following naturally from the previous (hence 'flow'). He compares it to playing jazz, when a musician doesn't think about what he's playing, but just gives himself up to the music. He never knows what's coming, but everything he plays is natural and right. In 'flow' we feel energized and alive, with a sense of control over our minds.

'Flow' activities have to be challenging, to involve some degree of skill and concentration (at least in the beginning, before they become effortless). As a result, passive activities like watching TV rarely induce the state. In a study of American teenagers, Csikszentmihalyi found that games and hobbies produced flow 39 percent of the time, compared to watching TV and listening to music 15 percent of the time. The activities that are most likely to create 'flow' are creative and challenging ones, like dancing or writing, playing chess, or the demanding or dangerous sporting activities I described earlier, like climbing or flying. If you're really lucky, you may have a job that gives you ready access to flow. You won't have much access to the state if you work in a call center or as a potato picker, but you might well do if you work as a teacher, a chef, a carpenter or a graphic artist. As a dancer described her experience of flow to Csikszentmihalyi: 'Your concentration is very complete. Your mind isn't wandering, you aren't thinking of something else; you are totally involved in what you are doing... You feel relaxed, comfortable, and energetic.'[4] Or as a mountaineer told him: 'When you're climbing... [it] becomes a world unto its own, significant only to itself. It's a concentration thing. Once you're into the situation, it's incredibly real and you're very much in charge of it.'[5]

According to Csikszentmihalyi, flow is one of the major sources of wellbeing in our lives. And significantly, his explanation of why it generates wellbeing is that it frees us from what he calls 'psychic entropy' – the normal random, uncontrollable chatter of the mind. In flow, our mind becomes quiet and we can control our own thoughts. We no longer have to think about things that we don't want to; in fact we don't even have to think at all.

In other words, in flow, humania is healed – temporarily, at least.

Meditation

Perhaps the most direct and effective way of temporarily healing humania, however, is through the practice of meditation. In fact, you could say that this is the very purpose of meditation (or at least one of them): to clear away our normal psychological discord so that we can experience harmony of being.

I'm sure that most readers of this book will already be familiar with the basic principles of meditation. Usually it means focusing your attention on an object – perhaps a word or group of words repeated silently in your mind (i.e. a mantra), a mental image or your own breathing. You close your eyes, sit quietly (often cross-legged, but not necessarily) and try to keep your attention fixed to the object. This sounds straightforward, but it's actually extremely difficult. When we meditate we realize just how crazy our minds are, and how little control we usually have over them. Sometimes you might find that there's so much thought-chatter that you can't focus your attention at all. Your thoughts are spinning so madly that it's like trying to steady a ship in a whirlwind. At other times, you might find that you can focus your attention for a few seconds, but then a new wave of thought arises and sweeps you away. Before you know it you're back in your office earlier today, or a few days ahead in the future, imagining what your weekend is going to be like.

Usually though, if you persevere and keep bringing your attention back to the mantra – or the image or your breathing – you find that your mind does begin to slow down. Your thoughts don't arise as rapidly and don't have the same power to sweep you away. Slowly you move toward a state of mental quietness and begin to feel a sense of inner wellbeing and wholeness. You start to feel comfortable in yourself; your being seems to open up, to become more spacious. At the same time, you might feel a subtle 'identity shift,' a sense that you've become a slightly different person, one who feels somehow more complete, more genuine and more grounded.

And then, when your meditation is over and you open your eyes and become aware of your surroundings again, you should feel a strong sense of presence. Everything around you seems more real and more beautiful and interesting. Colors seem brighter, objects seem more intricate and individual, and you notice patterns and objects that were there all along but somehow bypassed your attention. You might really *see* the pattern on a cup or a T-shirt for what seems like the first time or the pattern of sunlight on the floor, be awestruck by the beauty of your garden or of the sky. And at the same time, you don't feel detached from your environment. The boundary between you and 'it' seems to have become softer, so that there seems to be a smooth flow of communication between you and your surroundings.

I wrote earlier that being immersed in thought-chatter isn't so different from dreaming, and often, when

I'm meditating, I have a strong sense of 'waking up' in this way. My mental fog gradually disperses and after a while – perhaps ten minutes – there's a sudden shift. My awareness of my surroundings becomes much brighter and clearer. It's like an endless bright blue sky emerging from behind a wall of clouds, and I have a strong sense that this is the *right* form of awareness, my optimum and – at the same time – most natural state. By comparison, my normal state of mind seems limited and clouded.

Sources of harmony

So why exactly is it that we become free of humania in these moments? What is it about meditation, sex, climbing or running that generates harmony of being? Presumably it's the same – or at least a similar – psychological process operating in each case.

As I've hinted, the most important factor is that all of these activities provide a focus for the mind. There's a steady stream of attention directed at a particular object. In some activities, the focus is very strong, as in 'flow' activities. At other times, the focus is less conscious and more relaxed, as in running, swimming or walking in the countryside. But in both cases, this steady and prolonged focusing of attention has the effect of quieting our thought-chatter. This is because our thought-chatter is fuelled by the attention we give to it. Every mechanism needs some fuel to keep running, and the crazy thought-churning machine inside our heads feeds off attention. As long as we listen to it, and allow ourselves to get immersed in it, it will run on forever. But when we focus our attention away from it for a period of time – perhaps a minimum of five minutes – it begins to fade away, in the same way that a car grinds to a halt when it runs out of fuel.

This is shown very clearly by the following passage from the naturalist author Annie Dillard, describing what happened when she was tracking muskrat (a type of rodent), concentrating hard while following the animals and trying to observe them:

> *Even more than baseball, stalking is a game played in the actual present. At every second, the muskrat comes, or stays, or goes, depending on your skill.*
>
> *Can I stay still? It is astonishing how many people cannot, or will not, hold still. I could not, or would not, hold still for thirty minutes inside, but at the creek I slow down, center down and empty I am not excited: my breathing is slow and regular... Instead of going rigid, I go calm. I center down wherever I am; I find balance and repose. I retreat – not inside myself, but outside myself, so that I am a tissue of senses. Whatever I see is plenty, abundance. I am the skin of water the wind plays over: I am petal, feather, stone...*
>
> *I have done this sort of thing so often that I have lost self-consciousness about moving slowly and halting suddenly; it is second nature to me now. And I have often noticed that even a few minutes of this self-forgetfulness is tremendously invigorating.*[6]

When the mind is quiet in this way, we become free of both the disturbance and negativity of thought-chatter. We feel a sense of inner stillness because there literally *is* stillness inside us. Our being becomes calm, like the still surface of a lake. And this also means that the super-critical person inside our heads – who's always criticizing our behavior and reminding us of the things we should feel bad about in the past and worry about in the future – disappears. There's no one to make us feel guilty, to make us worry about the future or bitter about the past.

The quieting of thought-chatter has the effect of softening the boundaries of the ego. To a large degree, the ego itself is sustained by thinking. Thinking is what the ego does; your thought-chatter is the sound of the ego talking to itself. Every thought reinforces the ego a little, in the same way that exercise strengthens a muscle. Or from a slightly different perspective, since there is always an 'I' doing the thinking, and always something that you're thinking *about,* thought-chatter continually reinforces the I/it duality created by the ego. So when we focus our attention away from our thought-chatter for a long period, the boundaries of the ego soften, and we're no longer plagued by a sense of isolation and incompleteness. As a result, the division between the self and the activity we're doing fades away, as Csikszentmihalyi notes of flow. Or, in situations where our awareness is more diffuse, the division between the self and our surroundings begins to fade away. Duality begins to give way to oneness; observation is transcended by participation; fragmentation is transcended by wholeness. The nagging sense of lack we normally feel is taken away. There's a smooth fluid connection between ourself and our experience. We're like islands that appear to be separate – but then the sea level falls and we realize that we're actually part of the same landmass.

Another effect here is the heightening of perception that experiences of harmony usually bring (as I described above with meditation). This is the result of the extra mental energy available, now that the energy is no longer used up through thinking and maintaining the structure of the ego. Normally, as an energy-saving measure, our perceptions are fairly automatic; we put very little conscious effort into perceiving the objects around us and our surroundings in general. But in experiences of harmony, we don't need to conserve mental energy anymore, and so this extra energy is taken on by perception. Our perceptions are no longer automatic, and so the world becomes more real and alive to us.

Resting inside ourselves

Now that there's much less psychological discord inside us, we're no longer pushed out of ourselves into distractions. We're able to inhabit our own mental space, to exist inside ourselves at the same time as in the world and in the present. This is why we experience a sense of spaciousness and fullness – because we're able to 'go into' ourselves. Our thought-chatter takes place at the 'surface level' of our being, and forms a barrier that stops us going deeper. But when it fades away, we're able to enter into our own being, to go deep into ourselves, and so we feel more whole and more expansive. It's like walking out of a tiny cramped room into an open field.

We become aware that, although the surface of our being is filled with disturbance and negativity, underneath there is a deep reservoir of stillness and wellbeing. The surface of our being is like a rough sea, sweeping us to and fro and making us feel disoriented and anxious. But if you wear diving equipment and go beneath the surface, you're suddenly in the midst of endless silence and stillness.

At this deeper level we also become aware of an *energy* that fills our being – a rich and densely powerful energy that seems to be the source of our wellbeing. This is the radiance of consciousness, whose nature is wellbeing in the same way that wetness is the nature of water.

In other words, the contentment we feel in these states isn't just the absence of our normal discontent. That would only be a neutral state. This is a positive and powerful experience of wellbeing from the depths of our being. As soon as our normal discontent fades away, a deep contentment takes its place. It seems that there are two layers to our being: a shallow surface layer of discontent, and a deep underground layer of wellbeing.

I mentioned above that meditation can bring about an 'identity shift,' and this is true of any experience of harmony of being. Sex, long-distance running or music can also make you feel as if you've become a deeper and truer version of your self, a person who feels more authentically *you*. You feel that the person you were before – your normal self – was almost a kind of impostor, who hypnotized you into thinking he or she was the real you. Now you stand back from that self and realize that it was limited and false. In other words, the two layers of our being also manifest themselves in terms of identity. There appears to be a shallow surface layer – the normal ego-self – and a deeper, more fundamental self, the witnessing consciousness that Indian philosophy refers to as *atman.*

In these moments, the lack of discord inside us means that we're free from the compulsion to do and able to *be.* In fact, this ability to do nothing is one of the most pleasant aspects of harmony of being. We can sit down at the table or walk around the house, and be content just to be here. There's no impulse to turn on the TV or the radio, to reach for a magazine or to check your e-mail or to phone a friend for a chat.

One of the most striking things about this state is how *natural* it feels. There's a sense of coming home, returning to a state that is our natural birthright, as if we're experiencing our being as it was originally, before our minds became infected with humania.[7]

Permanent harmony

The importance of these experiences of harmony of being can't be overemphasized. These are the rare moments when we become truly sane, when the psychological can of worms inside us temporarily recedes, and we experience the wellbeing and wholeness of our deeper nature. These are the moments when we glimpse the natural wholeness and freshness experienced by young children, and the natural contentment and connection of indigenous peoples. In these moments, we become human *beings,* rather than human doings. Life suddenly ceases to be a struggle full of stress and discord, and is filled with a sense of ease.

Nevertheless, you could say that the problem with these experiences is that they are *just* experiences. They're just temporary. They might last for a few hours, but sooner or later ego-madness returns, like a headache a few hours after you've taken painkillers. At some point the mind starts chattering again, the walls of the ego grow strong and solid again, and our psychological discord re-emerges. Our normal state of being always seems to reestablish itself, as if it's a kind of 'mold' that our psyche has been set into. After feeling so free and so content and connected to your own self and the world around you, you're back in your ordinary world of worry and pressure.

But the important thing is that, as I inferred earlier, harmony doesn't *have* to be just temporary. In fact, since we've now identified the psychological conditions of temporary experiences, it's easy to see what the conditions of a permanent state would be: a state of permanent mental quietness, with no random thought-chatter running through our minds, so that there is no disturbance and negativity inside us. We would experience a permanent state of inner stillness and spaciousness. Our ego-structure would be permanently softened so that we wouldn't experience isolation and incompleteness. The ego would no longer be an isolated entity, but a permanent, integrated part of our being.

Over the next two chapters, we're going to investigate how we can generate this permanent change of being.

CHAPTER 10
Going Inside

One of the most exciting scientific developments in recent years is neuroplasticity (or neural plasticity, as it's sometimes called). Most scientists used to believe that once a person reached adulthood, their brain was fully formed and remained in the same basic state for the rest of their lives. The brain was fixed and 'hardwired' to do certain things and never changed, apart from injuries or illnesses, until it started to decay in old age. But thanks to modern brain-scanning technology, we now know that this isn't true. We now know that the brain is a marvelously pliable thing that is constantly growing and remolding itself.

This is how people recover from strokes. New brain cells are created and new connections are made between old cells. In addition, abilities and functions can shift to different, undamaged parts of the brain. For example, if the part of the brain that processes vision was damaged by the stroke, a different part of the brain can take over that role.

Something similar happens whenever we 'exercise' our brains. Neurogenesis – the creation of new brain cells – can occur when we take in new information, learn new skills or facts or when we test our memory, our powers of concentration or other cognitive skills. We can also create new 'neural networks' – groups of interconnected brain cells that work together – and alter the levels of different brain chemicals.

A 2005 study found that neurogenesis can occur very rapidly. A group of medical students' brains were scanned while they were studying for their exams. Within just a few months, the number of cells in the posterior and lateral parietal cortex – the part of the brain just behind the crown of the skull – had dramatically increased.[1]

Neuroplasticity shows that we are *in control* of our brains. We know that we're responsible for our bodies, that we have a choice whether to keep them fit and healthy or to let them degenerate. And we should think of our brains in the same way. We can *train* the brain to become more developed in certain areas, and to remain generally more alert and acute. Alternatively, we can allow the brain to 'wither' by failing to generate new cells and allowing neuronal circuits to weaken.

Massively significant though these findings are, they aren't so relevant to humania – which, after all, is a psychological rather than a neurological condition. What *is* relevant is a similar, parallel concept to neuroplasticity, which I call *'psycho*plasticity.' The concept here is that the *mind* – or psyche – is plastic and pliable in a similar way to the brain. In the same way that we can train the brain and change its structure, we can remold our own psyche.

Specifically, in relation to this book, it's possible for us to remold the psyche in such a way that we heal humania. We can heal the effects of traumatic experiences, and change the structure and functioning of the ego. The ego doesn't have to be such a dominant part of the psyche, with such strong boundaries. Our minds don't *have to* be filled with discord. It's possible for us to create a new kind of psyche.

Over the next two chapters, I'm going to suggest eight stages leading to this end. The stages are presented sequentially, but the sequence isn't rigid – in particular, the last three stages are fairly interchangeable and could be swapped around. The amount of time and effort you need to devote to each stage will vary according to your present psychological state. It may well be that you've done some work at the earlier stages already – for example, you may already be used to spending time with yourself, and have had some therapy to deal with the effects of trauma, or to train you to deal with negative thoughts. In that case, you should simply start at one of the later stages. It's up to you to decide where you're up to, and where you need to begin.

It's also important to bear in mind that the stages aren't strictly exclusive, but holistic. They aren't like rungs of a ladder but layers to be added, complementing each other. This means that you should continue with the earlier practices as you add the later ones to them, just as you would with the Eightfold Path of Buddhism or the Eight-limbed Path of Yoga. It also means that you don't need to feel that you've completely 'mastered' each stage before you move on to the next – it's enough for you to feel fairly confident, as if you've made some degree of progress. In fact, it's helpful for some stages to overlap. For example, once you move to Stage 7 (regular meditation) it will enhance the progress you've already made at Stages 3 and 4 (dis-identifying with thoughts and dealing with negative thought-patterns).

The preconditions of healing humania

Although not significant enough to be stages in themselves, there are two preconditions of healing humania. These are really the two preconditions of healing any illness or disorder. The first is simply to be aware that the illness *exists,* to realize that your symptoms can be traced back to a particular source and to identify it. This isn't so easy to do with humania – the condition is so close to us that it's hard to separate ourselves from it. It's difficult to see it as a problem because we *are* it. But after reading to this point, you should be well aware of it as a disorder!

The second precondition is having the courage to face up to humania, and to accept it as a problem. Many people try to cope with serious illness by ignoring the reality of their predicament. They convince themselves that it's not as serious as it seems, or avoid thinking about it altogether and immerse themselves in distractions and activities. But this doesn't help at all. It just suppresses fear rather than transcends it. The fear intensifies beneath the surface and bursts through at a later date.

It's easy to practice avoidance with humania – that's what most of us have been doing all our lives, after all. But it's similar to sensing that there is a problem in your marriage. It's tempting to just carry on as normal, to avoid the effort and upheaval of change, and hope that the problem will just fade away of its own accord. But the discord always remains beneath the surface. At some point, if you want to find harmony in your marriage again, you have to be brave enough to confront the problem and take measures to solve it.

Facing up to an illness or disorder is the point where the healing process can begin.

Stage 1: Turning your attention inside yourself

The first real stage toward cultivating a permanent state of harmony is to go *into* yourself. This sounds almost trite, but since most of us spend so much our lives living *outside* ourselves, it's by no means an easy task.

To some degree, this is a question of habit. We're so used to directing our attention outside ourselves, on activities, tasks and distractions that it feels alien to reverse our attention and look into our minds. The more we repeat an action – like smoking or gambling – the more its 'habitual power' builds up, until it becomes automatic, a fixed pattern of behavior that we have little or no control over. And since we've been repeating the action of turning our attention outside ourselves (in search of an object to immerse it in) dozens of times a day throughout our adult lives, its habitual power is enormous.

Another problem here is that, because we spend so much time outside ourselves, we aren't used to inhabiting our own mental space. When we go inside and touch into our psychological discord, part of the reason why it is so disturbing to us is simply that it's so unfamiliar. We're like a person who never leaves the suburbs and is shocked when they pay a visit to the city and experience its cacophonous chaos. This is one of the problems some people have when they first start meditating, particularly if the method they're taught is dense and demanding and they aren't given much guidance. They're amazed by the wildness of their own minds, by the myriad dizzy spinning thoughts that whiz through them. The chaos inside their minds scares them, and they often end the meditation feeling more anxious and unstable than when they started.

What we need to do is to make a conscious effort to spend time with our own selves, in our own mental space, even if at first this might be a little uncomfortable. This means weaning ourselves off distractions to some degree, trying to reduce the time we spend watching TV, surfing the Internet or shopping. It may mean not having the radio or CD player on in the background while you do the cooking or the dishes, not listening to your iPod as you walk to work, or writing texts or e-mails while you're on the subway or train. As with any addiction, it's sensible to do this gradually – not just in terms of time, but also by switching to less 'heavy-duty' distractions which are less absorbing. For example, you could reduce the time you spend watching TV shows or surfing the net and spend more time reading books and listening to music.

I also recommend taking up non-distracting activities that allow you to spend time within your own being. In fact, all of the harmony-generating activities we looked at in the last chapter can help us here – sports like running, swimming or climbing, walking in the countryside, or 'flow-inducing' creative activities like playing music, dancing, writing, painting, gardening, and so on. (Although not meditation at this point.)

This might mean taking a new attitude to enjoyment. Roughly speaking, there are two types of enjoyment. First, there's hedonistic enjoyment, which helps us to override or to divert ourselves from our psychological discord – drinking or taking drugs, shopping, eating junk food, going to nightclubs or parties or driving fast cars. Activities like these press instinctive 'pleasure buttons' inside us or produce pleasurable chemical changes. This kind of enjoyment can be powerful but it usually only lasts for a short time and often leaves us feeling worse than when we started.

The second type of enjoyment comes from the harmony-generating activities I mentioned earlier, such as sports, walking and creative pursuits. These bring happiness by transforming our being or altering the structure of our psyche. They don't help us to escape from our psychological discord, but enable us to *heal* it. The happiness these activities bring isn't chemical, but spiritual.

And so, in order to move toward harmony, it's important to become more oriented around the latter type of enjoyment. Of course, this doesn't mean that you should live like a monk, and never enjoy good food, wine and socializing. (I certainly enjoy these things too.) It's a question of moderation, and also of the attitude with which you approach these activities. Eating and socializing can be either hedonistic or harmony-generating activities, depending on your attitude toward them. If you eat food slowly and quietly, it can be a powerful meditative exercise; and if you meet other people with openness, attention and empathy, human contact can be a powerful experience of connection, a transcendence of ego-separation.

At the same time as generating temporary states of harmony, activities like these weaken the psychic habit of focusing outside ourselves, and help to create a *new* habit of resting inside our mental space. We're like travelers in a foreign country, and in order to start a new life there, we first need to acclimatize ourselves.

Stage 2: Dealing with trauma

However, since it's our psychological discord that impels us to focus our attention outside ourselves in the first place, we also need to find ways of alleviating it. To continue the metaphor I used earlier, a teenager who spends all her time outdoors because of the terrible atmosphere at home will only be able to start spending time at home once the atmosphere there becomes more harmonious. We can only begin to feel comfortable within our own mental space once the discord had faded away to some degree.

If you've been through traumatic experiences in the past, it's likely that these have intensified the 'base level' of your psychological discord, so you should begin by focusing on this trauma. While you carry the residual pain of traumatic experiences inside you, or if they have damaged the structure of your psyche, it will be very difficult to generate inner harmony until the effects are healed to some degree, through therapy.

One of the most effective ways of healing trauma is a relatively new therapy called Eye Movement Desensitization and Reprocessing (EMDR), developed over the last two decades by psychologist Francine Shapiro. The basic principle of the therapy is that traumatic experiences are so overwhelming that the mind can't process them properly. Rather than going into our main memory system, they are separated into their own memory network, where they can't be rationalized or consciously processed. They are stored in a dysfunctional way, which becomes a source of anxiety and psychological pain.

The aim of EMDR is to help the client process these traumatic memories, and so reduce their painfulness. In an EMDR session, the client is asked to create a visual image associated with the traumatic experience, while their eyes follow the therapist's finger moving back and forth. (For reasons that aren't fully clear, it appears that sweeping eye movements reduce stress and anxiety.) At the same time, the therapist encourages the client to 'reframe' the experience, making it more familiar and comfortable, and less threatening. As a result, the client becomes desensitized to the experience. It's also believed that once the traumatic experience is 'unlocked' from its own isolated memory network, it links up with other, conscious memory networks, which also helps it to become less threatening.

EMDR sounds almost absurdly simple, but it has had such good results that the US government has approved it as treatment for post-traumatic stress disorder in war veterans. It has also been very effective in healing trauma following natural disasters and terrorist attacks. Usually, it takes just a few sessions for clients to report that the memory of the original traumatic experience is no longer causing them pain.

Another technique that has had good results in dealing with trauma is Exposure Therapy. In this method, clients relive their traumatic experiences, and so gradually become desensitized toward them. This can be done through visualization, or by talking through the experience in the present tense, as if it's happening now. While the client relives the experience, the therapist guides them through relaxation exercises, and encourages them to 'reframe' their thoughts about the experience, trying to dispel negative thoughts and feelings.

This can also be done through virtual reality, where the client is exposed to sounds, smells, and sights associated with the traumatic experience. For example, a war veteran will be exposed to the sound of bombs and bullets, and the smell of fire. This exposure is repeated many times, until the client becomes 'habituated' to the experience, and no longer feels any negative emotions.

A similar and equally effective approach is Acceptance and Commitment Therapy (ACT). This encourages a client to face up to their traumatic experiences, to accept rather than avoid them. The client is asked to examine the negative thoughts and beliefs associated with their trauma, while the therapist helps them to realize that these thoughts and beliefs are not *them* – that is, that the client has an identity apart from them, and can observe and control the thoughts. Once the client can see how the beliefs are affecting their life, they can begin to change them. At this point, they commit to a process of transforming their beliefs and improving their quality of life.

Other therapies have been shown to be effective in healing trauma, including Peter Levine's Somatic Experiencing and Cognitive Behavioral Therapy (CBT) itself (of which all the above therapies contain elements). There may well be one particular therapy that suits you best, or which is best suited to the type of trauma you've experienced (obviously, some types of trauma – such as sexual abuse – won't be suited to Exposure Therapy, for example). With such a wide variety of effective therapies available, there's no reason at all why we should think of ourselves as helpless victims of trauma. It's true that trauma can cause major psychological damage, but because of the plasticity of the psyche, this damage can be healed with surprising ease and speed.

Brain scans have shown how quickly therapy can change the form and functioning of the brain, through neural plasticity. For example, the American psychiatrist Dr. Jeffrey M. Schwartz (of the UCLA School of Medicine) gave therapy to patients suffering from obsessive-compulsive disorders, and scanned their brains before and afterward. After the therapy, the brains scans showed that the part of the brain associated with obsessive behavior – the caudate nucleus – was less active.[2]

And if these changes can happen on a neurological level, they can obviously happen on a psychological level too.

Stage 3: Stepping back from thought

Once you've begun to learn the habit of looking inside yourself, and once you're no longer so disabled by traumatic experiences, the next stage is to try to reduce the cognitive discord caused by your thoughts. Thought-chatter is a problem *in itself,* since it creates a constant disturbance inside us, and the *negative tone* of so much of the chatter is a problem too, since this generates negative emotions and moods.

As I suggested earlier, to a large extent this negative tone is due to the anxious atmosphere created by our ego-separateness. However, many of our negative thought-patterns are also learned, passed on to us by our parents, or developed in response to our experiences. If we could change our relationship to these negative thoughts, or change the thoughts *themselves,* this would decrease our psychological discord further, and make it easier still for us to live inside ourselves.

The most important thing we need to learn in relation to our thought-chatter is to 'dis-identify' with it. Normally we're immersed in our thoughts, and our identity is bound up with them. To paraphrase the philosopher Descartes (who wrote 'I think, therefore I am'), we *are* what we think. We allow our thoughts to dictate our moods. For example, if you think a negative thought – e.g. 'Oh no, I've got to go to that boring meeting tomorrow,' or 'Why do bad things always happen to me? It's as if the world has got a grudge against me' – there will be a slight dip in your mood. If you think a large number of negative thoughts then you may become slightly depressed. And if you habitually think negative thoughts such as those described above, you're likely to suffer from depression.

Alternatively, if you think positive thoughts – e.g. 'Brilliant – I'm going away in two weeks' or 'I did really well at work today' – then there will be a slight upswing in your mood. And if you're a habitual positive thinker, then you're likely to be a generally happy person.

Thoughts can create other moods too. If you think about a recent episode when someone treated you badly, you become angry; if you replay the memory of a golden opportunity you didn't take you may become bitter and regretful, and so on. If you habitually focus on negative past events in this way, other people might see you as a generally 'angry' or 'bitter' person.

Everyone's thought-chatter has a different tone and a different nature. Your thinking could generally be optimistic or pessimistic, anxious or confident, self-critical or self-supporting, and so on. You have certain 'core' attitudes to yourself which are expressed through your thinking, and which originate from your parents' attitude to when you were a child and your other life experiences. (To a lesser extent, they might be the result of biological inheritance too, e.g. your innate personality – if there is such a thing – might naturally tend toward pessimism or optimism, or to depression or happiness.) If you had a difficult childhood and have been through other painful experiences, these core attitudes might be verbalized as 'I don't deserve to be happy,' or 'Whatever I do, it's bound to go wrong.' Or if you had a happy childhood, and generally positive experiences since then, you're more likely to have positive core attitudes, which might be verbalized as 'I expect to be happy and to achieve what I set out to do.' And so it's easy to see how habitual thought-patterns can go a long way to determining your personality: whether you're confident or shy, laid back or anxious, happy or depressive, and so on.

However, we need to learn that, no matter how powerful they are, these thoughts *aren't us.* As the Acceptance and Commitment Therapy discussed above teaches, the real 'you' stands apart from your thoughts, like a person on a riverbank watching the river flow by. Normally we're *in* the river, carried away by our thoughts, but we need to learn to step *out* of the river. As deep meditation makes us aware, we actually consist of two identities: the thought-created personality, and the essence or consciousness that can observe the thought-created personality and is still conscious even when that personality is in abeyance (such as in meditation or deep sleep). In spiritual traditions this is sometimes called the 'witness,' or referred to as 'Self.' In the ancient Indian spiritual texts the *Upanishads,* the two selves are compared to two birds that sit in the same tree, one of which 'eats the fruit thereof' while the other 'looks on in silence.'

What we need to do, in effect, is to transfer the locus of our identity from the thinking self to the observing self. This can happen very suddenly, especially in times of great turmoil, when the thought-created self becomes so riddled with negative thoughts and emotions that it feels the impulse to destroy itself. This is what happened to the spiritual teacher and author Eckhart Tolle when he was on the point of killing himself, following a long period of anxiety and depression. As he recounts in *The Power of Now*, the thought 'I cannot live with myself any longer,' kept running through his mind. Suddenly he became aware of the duality this thought implied, between the 'I' and the 'myself' it couldn't live with. He became aware that there were two identities inside him, and immediately his identity withdrew from the thought-created self. He realized his identity as the deeper, observing self. His suffering ego-self dissolved, and the observing self became his normal, permanent self.

In *Out of the Darkness*, I tell the story of Ken Baldwin, who attempted to commit suicide by jumping off the Golden Gate Bridge in San Francisco. As soon as he jumped, he shifted out of his identification with his suffering ego, and all its negative thoughts. It was as if a thick mental fog suddenly disappeared. He immediately knew that he didn't want to die, and that 'Everything in my life that I'd thought was unfixable was totally fixable – except for having just jumped.' Fortunately he was one of the very few people who have survived jumping off the bridge, and had the opportunity to begin his life anew.

To a large extent though, we can train ourselves to dis-identify with our thought-chatter. One way of doing this is through *Vipassana* meditation. Whereas most types of meditation aim to quiet the mind, the aim of *Vipassana* is simply to *observe,* to stand apart from the flow of our experience and watch the arising and passing away of thoughts, emotions and perceptions. In this way, *Vipassana* trains us to dis-identify with thoughts and emotions, and to identify more with the witness. (In this sense, *Vipassana* is perhaps better seen as a type of *mindfulness* than meditation. I will discuss the differences between mindfulness and meditation shortly.)

You can also practice a less formal type of *Vipassana.* For example, when you're lying in bed at night or in the morning, just spend a few minutes observing the flow of your thoughts. As you do so, be aware of how your thoughts try to 'pull you in.' It's a little like being at a party and feeling pulled into an interesting conversation – a part of you wants to become immersed in it, and feels like you're missing something by letting it pass by. But make a mental effort to hold back. If you resist the temptation to go with the thought, it will quickly pass by – whereas if you latch on to it, your attention will give it fuel, and it will quickly mutate into a dozen different thoughts, spinning off in different directions and taking you with them.

Another useful exercise is to trace your thoughts back, as I described in Chapter 2. Even if you can't stop yourself latching on to your thoughts, and they do end up carrying you away, when a train of thoughts comes to an end, trace it back to its starting point, and back through all the points that took you from there to here. You'll probably be amazed at the twists and turns your thoughts have taken in a short space of time, how they jump from one topic to another with no rhyme or reason, as if they have a will of their own. But most importantly, this will help to create a distance between you and your thoughts, and help you develop the habit of observing them.

Dis-identifying with our thoughts reduces psychological discord in two ways. First, since thought-chatter is no longer being fuelled by your attention and absorption, it loses its impetus, and becomes quieter. Just *being aware* of your thoughts, rather than being immersed in them, reduces their power.

Second, once you've learned to stand back and observe your thoughts, you've gone some way to breaking the link between thoughts and feelings. Being aware of a thought as it arises, and standing apart from it rather than becoming immersed in it, means that it's much less likely to trigger negative feelings. For example, if a thought pops up about a talk you have to do in a couple of weeks, it's less likely to trigger anxiety, or if a memory arises of a negative event from the past, it's likely to trigger feelings of humiliation or regret. Again, just being aware of this process weakens its effect. Your observing self can tell you, *Hold on, this is just a thought, I don't have to pay attention to it.* The thought has less power to affect you, just like criticism from a person whose opinion you don't respect.

Stage 4: Transcending negative thought-patterns

Once you've dis-identified with your thoughts to some degree, you can begin the process of *changing* the way you think. Because of the anxious atmosphere of the separate ego, and because most of our parents suffered from humania and so passed on *their* negative attitudes to us, almost all of us have picked up some negative cognitive habits. These are often so deeply ingrained that they're difficult to see, but may manifest themselves as slight shyness, insecurity, anxiety or mistrust. Alternatively, they may manifest themselves in strategies we use to compensate for them – for example, in arrogance, narcissism or an overbearing personality. But once the negative beliefs and thoughts behind these traits are unearthed, they are surprisingly easy to change. This is one of the benefits of psychoplasticity. Because the psyche is so pliable, new cognitive habits can replace old ones very quickly.

This is the whole purpose of Cognitive Behavioral Therapy. The great insight of CBT is that it's not so much the events or experiences of our lives that make us unhappy or happy, but the way we interpret and think about them. (To quote Shakespeare's phrase in *Hamlet*, 'There is nothing either good or bad, but thinking makes it so.') Negative thoughts create negative moods, and positive thoughts create positive moods. When any event happens to us, our cognitive biases and attitudes often determine whether we view it in a positive or a negative light.

Often what we think of as problems are just neutral events – and potentially even positive ones – cast in a negative light by our thoughts. For example, if you're asked to do a presentation at work, you may see it as a problem and worry about it for days in advance. But another person might view it positively and look forward to it as an opportunity to put forward their views and show off their knowledge. Or if you receive an invitation to go to a friend's wedding, you might think, *How wonderful! It'll be great to see all my old friends again!* Whereas another person might think, *Oh no – now Sally's getting married, and I'm still single! All my friends are married now. It's humiliating!* A couple of years ago, it was my wife's 40th birthday and a few of her friends came round for breakfast. One of her friends said, 'I can't believe we're 40 now! How depressing – we're getting old!' However, my wife's friend Kerry is from South Africa, where some of her friends and relatives died in their 20s and 30s. So her attitude to aging was different. 'I don't find it depressing,' she replied. 'I'm just glad I've made it to the age of 40!'

This suggests that the best way to deal with what appear to be problems is not necessarily to focus on changing our lives, but on changing our *thinking.* If you aren't happy in your relationship, you first instinct may be to end it, and look for a new partner. But before you do that, it may be worth exploring how your thoughts about yourself – and your partner – are affecting the relationship. The same with your job, or if you aren't happy with your appearance or the house you live in. It may well be that you have real problems, genuine reasons for discontent – such as an abusive partner or an unfulfilling job that doesn't suit you – so that you really should look to end the relationship or look for a better job. But it's also very possible that the *real* problem lies not so much with the situations themselves but with your attitude and beliefs toward them.

In CBT, the therapist and client work together to uncover distorted thoughts and attitudes. For example, they might find that the client always expects the worst, with an underlying script saying something like, 'The world has got it in for me – everything I do goes wrong eventually.' There might be negative scripts the client has absorbed from their parents, such as 'I don't deserve love,' 'People don't like me,' or 'Other people shouldn't be trusted.' Together, they might find that the client has very thin skin, constantly interpreting other people's actions as slights against them, or they might work together to deal with fears and phobias, such as fear of flying or spiders.

Once they've uncovered these negative thought processes, the therapist and client try to replace them with alternative explanations and beliefs. For example, to deal with the script 'The world has got it in for me,' the client will come up with evidence against this idea, recalling situations when things have gone well for them, and making a list of them. Or if their problem is a thin skin, the therapist will encourage them to 'depersonalize' the situation, to take the perspective of other people and realize that what seem to be 'slights' are often just forgetfulness or ignorance. For example, if someone ignores you and you feel offended, perhaps it was just that the person was in a rush, or they didn't even see you. And even if the person was genuinely rude or disrespectful to you, there could be reasons for this too: perhaps they're jealous of you, or feel threatened.

CBT is sometimes criticized for the amount of 'homework' it involves, such as making lists of evidence for and against beliefs or keeping thought records. However, these are necessary to reinforce new thought-patterns and to replace the old negative cognitive habits with new positive ones.

Another criticism sometimes leveled at CBT is that it only brings about superficial and short-term change. Some psychologists argue that it should be combined with deeper therapies (such as person-centered or psychodynamic therapy) to achieve long-lasting effects. Nevertheless, there is impressive evidence for CBT's effectiveness. For example, in a recent study, people suffering from 'pathological perfectionism' (who set impossibly high standards for themselves and feel a constant sense of failure and anxiety as a result) were given a 12-week course of CBT, and their brain activity was measured before and after. The researchers found that the therapy caused significant changes in the cortex of the brain. Compared to a control group, the participants had a significantly higher level of 'cortical inhibition,' and also showed a decrease in anxiety and in automatic thoughts.[3] (Of course, this study is another example of how rapidly neuroplasticity can work too.)

I've also found evidence of the effectiveness of cognitive exercises myself. For four years, I taught courses on the psychology of happiness with adult students at the University of Manchester. We tried out various exercises to enhance our wellbeing, and there were two that stood out as being the most effective. One was writing an 'appreciation list.' I wrote down the beginnings to some sentences on the whiteboard and asked my students to complete them in their own words: 'I'm glad I'm not...'; 'I appreciate my...'; 'I'm glad I'm...'; and 'I'm fortunate because...' After they had discussed their sentences with their partners, I gave them each a sheet of colored card and some pens, and asked them to write an 'appreciation list' with at least eight of these sentences, or variations of them.

At the end of the session, I told them to pin up the list at home, in a place where they could read it every day – on the kitchen wall, in the hall, even in the toilet. It was important to spend at least five minutes each day reading through the list and digesting the meaning of the sentences. Most of the students stuck to this, and at the end of the course, four weeks later, they all felt it had a made a big difference to their outlook and their mood. They all felt much more appreciative and generally happier. I made contact with some of them several months later, and most told me that they felt this appreciative attitude had become habitual, so that they always had a fundamental sense of the value of a lot of things that they used to take for granted, such as their health, their friends and relatives, their freedom and prosperity, and life itself.

However, the most effective exercise was one in which I focused on different types of negative feelings: fear/anxiety, guilt, jealousy/desire, insecurity, and bitterness/resentment. I gave the students a worksheet with three different columns on it. I asked them to think of one or two situations where they experienced the above feelings, and to describe the situation briefly in the first column. Then, in the next column, I asked them to verbalize the thoughts they had in these situations. For example, if they wrote, 'I feel guilty about letting my friend down when he was in need,' the thought might be something like, 'I'm so selfish – I should be ashamed of myself.' Or if they wrote, 'There's someone at work who doesn't like me' as an example of insecurity, the thought might be 'I'm a boring person. Other people usually don't like me.'

Next, I asked the students to imagine that they had a very wise friend, who was going to give them sound advice to counteract these negative thoughts. I asked them to write this advice in the third column. So the 'counteractive thought' to 'I should be ashamed of myself' might be 'The past is over – I can only learn from it and do better.' Or to 'Other people usually don't like me' it might be 'There are lots of people who do like me – and if some people don't, that's only natural

– you can't expect everyone to like you.' Or 'As long as I like myself, it doesn't matter what other people think.'

Finally, once they had written down wise and rational counteractive thoughts to all their negative thoughts, I asked them to take a new sheet of paper and write down all of the 'counteractive' thoughts in a list. This became a list of 'affirmations,' which was specific to them, focused on their particular negative thoughts. They went through the lists with their partners, and at the end of the session, I asked them to make a habit of talking through the list for a few minutes every morning before breakfast, or to say it aloud to themselves as they were driving.

I'm dubious about some types of affirmations, particularly the 'law of attraction' type, where people think they can get anything they want in life just by verbalizing and visualizing it. This strikes me as a bizarre form of narcissism and wish fulfillment. But as long as they're realistic and tailored to your particular characteristics and needs, affirmative statements can be very effective as a way of reinforcing positive thoughts, and creating new cognitive habits. A 1980 study by psychologists in New Zealand, for example, found that reciting affirmations for ten minutes each morning for two weeks increased people's happiness by 25 percent. In this case, it's significant that the affirmations were specific and not overly ambitious – for example, 'I have confidence in my decisions,' 'I have a feeling that the future is going to bring good things,' 'I accept the fact that I have my weaknesses, but I can do something about them,' and 'I get a lot of pleasure out of everything I do.'[4] On the other hand, a recent study found that when people with low self-esteem repeated a vague positive affirmation for several minutes

('I am a lovable person'), it actually decreased their self-esteem.[5] This shows the importance of using affirmations in the right way.

My students certainly found this exercise effective – at the end of the session where we initially did it, there was a fantastic mood in the classroom, as they all felt an immediate lift from the affirmations. And many of them told me that this positive attitude persisted over the following weeks.

More empirically, when I was teaching six- or eight-week courses (as opposed to the two-day workshops I sometimes ran), in the first week I would ask the students to rate their general level of wellbeing, between one and ten. (The actual question I asked was 'In general, how happy or unhappy do you feel?') Alongside the ratings were descriptors, so that zero was 'extremely unhappy', five was 'neutral', six was 'slightly happy,' and ten was 'extremely happy.' I would also ask the questions, 'On average, what percentage of the time do you feel happy? What percentage of the time do you feel unhappy? What percentage of the time do you feel neutral?' Here I asked them to make sure that the percentages added up to 100. (These questionnaires were developed by Dr. Michael Fordyce, one of the pioneers into research on happiness and wellbeing.) I would take away their responses, and then at the end of the six or eight weeks, I would ask the students the same questions (without giving them reference to their original answers) and compare the figures to the original ones.

In total, I ran four happiness courses, each six or eight weeks long, with groups of between 12 and 20 adults. And in every case, there was a significant increase in the students' level of happiness, on both scores. On the first questionnaire, the most significant was an increase of an average score of 6.8 to 8.3, while the least significant was an increase from 7.0 to 7.9. This suggests that the above two exercises – combined with others, which I don't have space to describe – had a real effect.

Because the psyche is so pliable, it may only take a few weeks for new cognitive habits to become habitual. In other words, after a while you may not consciously need to think positively anymore – to read through your appreciation list or a list of affirmations – because those positive attitudes will now be ingrained. Thinking positively will be automatic to you. This is why CBT can be effective so quickly – usually six to eight weekly sessions are seen as sufficient.

The popular idea that it only takes 21 days to form a new habit may be a slight exaggeration. In a 2009 study at University College London, 96 people were tracked as they tried to learn new habits, such as eating a piece of fruit with lunch, drinking a glass of water or going for a 15-minute run every day. On average, it took 66 days for the behavior to become automatic to them[6]. But 66 days is still not long, especially when the effects of changing your thinking are so great – less psychological discord, enhanced wellbeing and therefore a greater ability to live inside ourselves.

There is certainly a limit to the effectiveness of cognitive approaches like these however. Teachers of positive thinking of CBT sometimes see creating a positive frame of mind as the ultimate goal, but it's only really an intermediate point. Thinking is still thinking, even if it's positive. Changing the way we think is a major step toward wellbeing, but an even greater step is to go *beyond thought* altogether. When there is no thought in our minds at all – or at least significantly less than normal – we feel a deeper kind of happiness, a positive mood that isn't triggered by thoughts, but which stems from a deep source of natural wellbeing inside us. And paradoxically, one of the major benefits of positive thinking is that it makes it easier for us to do this. It helps to make us comfortable in our mental space – so comfortable that we can empty our minds completely. This is one of the aims of meditation, which we will look at shortly. However, there are two further practices we need to add to our lives before then.

CHAPTER 11

Cultivating Inner Harmony

People who follow paths of personal or spiritual development are sometimes accused of selfishness. They're preoccupied with their own wellbeing instead of other people's, the argument goes. They shut themselves away, meditating with their eyes closed, rather than engaging with the world, and trying to change it for the better.

I don't think this is wholly valid. It's true that some spiritual seekers retire to monasteries and ashrams, or treat the everyday world as an illusion that is of no consequence. One of the most extreme examples of this was the Indian mystic Ramakrishna who, when asked about the value of social action, said, 'Hospitals, dispensaries, and all such things are unreal. God alone is real... Why should we forget him and lose ourselves in too many activities?'[1]

In most cases, however, spiritual development makes people less self-centered and more connected. It generates more empathy and a greater concern for social and global problems. For every solitary hermit, there has been a 'spiritual activist' who has devoted most of his or her life to serving others. Although some of them went through periods of solitary 'spiritual training' early on, mystics such as St. Teresa of Avila, St. Catherine of Siena, the Baal Shem Tov (founder of Hasidic Judaism), George Fox, Vivekananda,

Gandhi – and many others – lived lives of great altruism, campaigning against injustice and oppression, trying to alleviate suffering and improve the predicaments of the oppressed and poor.

As we have seen, a lack of empathy – and a consequent lack of altruism – is one of the characteristics of humania. Our strong ego-boundary 'walls us off' from other people, preventing us from making an empathic connection with them. In addition, our preoccupation with our own psychological discord makes it difficult for us to 'step outside' ourselves. We're too immersed in our own problems to worry about other people's. In philosopher Ken Wilber's terms, we have an 'egocentric' outlook rather than a wider sociocentric or worldcentric perspective that generates a concern for social or global issues, or the desire to 'make the world a better place.'

As a result, once you've healed the effects of trauma to some degree, and begun to transcend negative thought-patterns, you'll find yourself naturally becoming more empathic and altruistic. As you become less immersed in your own subjective world of discord, you'll reach out into other people's mind-space. You'll become able to 'feel with' them, to sense their suffering or happiness as if it were your own.

Stage 5: Service

But at the same time, it's important to think of service – performing altruistic acts – as a developmental practice that we can consciously use as way of healing our minds. Acts of service help us to transcend separation. They help increase our empathic connection with other people, and so soften our ego-boundaries. They help us to sense our real identity as part of an ocean of shared consciousness, rather than as islands of individual consciousness, each at the center of the universe. When we serve other people – act altruistically to try to alleviate their suffering, improve their predicament or further their development – we don't just connect with them, but with a transcendent dimension of oneness that lies behind all seeming separateness. And the more we connect with this dimension, the less self-centered and separate we become.

If you have young children or elderly parents, or if you work as a nurse, counselor or teacher, you may already be using service as a developmental practice, even without realizing it. If not, try taking on some voluntary work for a charity or community organization, a local hospice, hospital or homeless people's hostel, a group that helps the elderly people in your neighborhood, or a conservation group. Or perhaps you could serve the whole human race in a more abstract way, through environmental, social or political social activism, trying to alleviate some of the oppression and discord that fills our world.

And after all, it's only fitting that we should try to heal the world, after collectively mistreating it for so long. The world needs all the altruism we can give it, because of the havoc that humania has wreaked on it, through thousands of years of conflict, oppression and inequality. We have a collective *duty* to try to alleviate suffering in the world. And it's also somehow fitting that, in the process of helping to alleviate the suffering of others, we also help to heal the suffering inside ourselves.

Stage 6: Conscious attention

Wherever we are and whatever we're doing, there are always three different things we can do with our attention: we can give it to the thought-chatter in our heads, we can immerse it in tasks or distractions, or we can focus it on the present, on our surroundings and experience. For example, if you're in the doctor's waiting room, you can daydream (perhaps think about what you're going to do at the weekend or mull over some problems you have at work), immerse your attention in a magazine, or observe the other people around you and the objects and décor of the room itself. Or when you go for a jog, you can daydream, listen to an audio book on your iPod, or give your attention to your surroundings, the scenery you pass and the nature around you. In shorthand, you can think of these three states as 'the three As': abstraction (i.e. immersion in thought-chatter), absorption (i.e. in activities or distractions), and attention (i.e. conscious attention to our experience).

It isn't cut and dried, of course – in a state of abstraction or absorption, you're usually in a state of *partial* attention too. For example, even if you're daydreaming or listening to an audio book while jogging, you're obviously still attentive to your surroundings to a *degree* – enough to pay attention to the traffic, or to keep to your normal route. But usually this is only a very basic and functional attention; the largest proportion of your mental energy is given up to absorption or abstraction.

Every moment of our lives, we unconsciously evaluate these three options and choose one of them. Normally we choose one of the first two As, of course, and enter into internal or external 'elsewhereness.' But after the previous five stages, you should find yourself spending more time in the third state. As your psychological discord decreases – and as you become more used to your own mental space and less dependent on distractions – you'll naturally find it easier to pay conscious attention to your experience. But like service, conscious attention should also be a practice in itself, and a habit that can be cultivated and encouraged.

This means making a conscious effort to focus your attention on the here and now. Whenever you realize that you're elsewhere, try to make a habit of bringing yourself back to the present. Whenever you realize that you've become immersed in thought-chatter, withdraw your attention from it and re-focus on your surroundings and your experience. Focus on the room you're in and the objects and other people around you, and on the sounds you can hear. Look at the color and shape of the objects and their relationship to each other. Feel the texture of the table you're sitting at, the pen you're using or the carpet under your feet. Make a conscious effort to use your sense of *smell* – perhaps the room or the street is filled with smells you weren't aware of. Do the same whenever you feel the impulse to immerse your attention in distractions or activities.

It's important to remember to do this gently. Don't *jolt* your attention away from thought-chatter – if you do, you'll generate resistance, which will make it difficult for you to be present. Presence can't work with forced attention, but only with relaxed and natural awareness. Rather than forcing yourself, just gently guide yourself back into the present, and reorientate yourself there. It's like walking in the park with a toddler who doesn't understand the concept of a straight line and keeps veering off the path in different directions: every few steps you have to gently pick him up and point him in the right direction.

For example, when you're walking to the train in the morning with your mind buzzing with thoughts about what happened last night or what's ahead of you today – give yourself a gentle mental nudge and bring your attention away from those thoughts and into the present. Transfer your attention away from your thought-chatter toward the sky above you, the trees and buildings, and the cars around you, and the awareness of yourself inside your body, walking in the midst of these surroundings. When you're eating your evening meal and realize that you're reading a newspaper, give yourself a mental nudge and transfer your attention to the taste of the food and the chewing and swallowing. Or when you're in a meeting at work: take your attention out of the discussion for a moment and be aware of the room you're in, take in its shape and its colors and its furniture. Be aware of yourself sitting there, of your bottom against the surface of the chair, your back against its back, and your feet on the floor.

We usually assume that activities like driving or eating or cooking aren't enough in themselves, because they're essentially mundane and dreary. We feel as though we need to combine them with distractions – like reading the paper while you eat or having the TV on in the kitchen while you cook – to make them more bearable. But when we do actually give ourselves wholly to the activities we find the opposite: these activities *are* sufficient in themselves; in fact, they provide a sense of ease and harmony that no distraction or daydream ever could.

With conscious attention the whole world becomes much more fascinating and beautiful. We realize that objects and scenes are only beautiful or fascinating in proportion to how much attention we give to them. Beauty isn't just something innate, a quality that some objects possess – much more than that it's something that we *create*. The more attention we invest, the more beauty and fascination we perceive. Everyday objects and scenes only seem mundane because we don't give them real attention. When we do consciously attend to them, we realize that they're just as attractive as ancient artifacts that we go to museums to look at, or unfamiliar foreign scenes that we travel across the world to see.

Once you get into the habit of bringing yourself back to the present you'll be surprised how easy it is to do. It quickly begins to feel natural, making our normal state of abstraction seem absurd. Why should I let these crazy whirls of memory and association take up my attention when there is this endlessly rich and intricate world in front of me, filled with layer after layer of is-ness and wonder? You might ask yourself. Being immersed in thought-chatter instead of giving your attention to your experience is like traveling to a beautiful city – such as Paris or Venice – and spending all your time there in your hotel room watching TV.

Conscious attention in relationships

It's especially important to practice conscious attention in our relationships. Often we don't give the people we're with our full attention or communicate with them properly because we're partially elsewhere. Particularly when we've been friends or partners with people for a long time and take them for granted, we let thought-chatter immerse our attention while we're talking with them – or even more blatantly, give part of our attention to the radio or TV. Your wife might be telling you about the terrible day she's had at work, but she's said similar things to you a hundred times before and you're busy thinking about the football match you're going to watch on TV later, or about what you've got to do at work tomorrow. The person you've sat next to at work for the last three years is telling you about the vacation he's booked for the summer, but you've always found him a bit boring and just automatically nod while daydreaming about the new girl on reception downstairs.

Many couples who have been together a long time are like this. They've known each other for so long that they no longer make the effort to listen to each other. They automatically switch off their attention, assuming that there is nothing new or interesting the other person can say. As a result, they become strangers to each other. They no longer share their thoughts and feelings; there's no exchange of ideas, feelings and energy, and so no real relationship. There's always a barrier between them – the barrier of their thought-chatter, on both sides. As a result, their selves never truly *meet* each other.

This creates discord in relationships. If you're largely elsewhere when you're with your partner or friends, you're unconsciously telling them that you don't value them. They will sense this, and feel insecure and demeaned as a result, which will lead to resentment and hostility.

If two people are largely elsewhere to each other, it also means that they don't genuinely know each other, in the same way that we don't genuinely know ourselves. They don't communicate intimately and directly, but only through their surface egos, without revealing their true selves. And this can lead to discord because it creates misunderstanding and mistrust. If you don't truly know someone, it's easy to misinterpret their actions and intentions, and you can never be completely sure of their feelings toward you.

Once you've begun to transcend humania, you'll find yourself naturally being more present to the people around you, as you will to life in general. But again, it's also worth practicing this consciously. When you're with you partner, your friends and colleagues, make a conscious effort to be present. Make the effort to be truly alone with them with no noise or distractions around you, with the TV and radio turned off and no newspapers or magazines to distract you. Try to give them your whole attention, reminding yourself not to take this person for granted, and that their every thought or feeling is as valuable as your own. Being nakedly alone with the person might feel uncomfortable at first, in the same way that inactivity, silence and solitude may feel uncomfortable. But once you establish a real connection with the person and begin to feel an exchange of empathy, this unease will fade away.

And this applies to the people who aren't so close to us too. The store assistant, the cab driver, the receptionist, the waitress or the person sitting next to you on the train – try to give them your complete attention. Be receptive and respectful to them, rather than treating them like objects. Even very brief contact with someone can create an empathic bond.

Relationships often have a power dynamic to them. One party is often in a superior position to the other. For example, a teacher usually feels he is in a dominant position to his students, a manager feels she is superior to her workers, a passenger in a taxi feels he has higher status than the driver, and so on. In sexual relationships, one partner may feel dominated by the other, or the relationship itself may be a constant power struggle, with one or both partners feeling belittled or mistreated and fighting to bend each other's will to their own. Even with friends and colleagues, we often feel that there are people who have stronger, more confident personalities than us and who make us feel inferior, while there are others we feel very confident with as if we're dominant toward them.

But when we're fully present to other people, this power dynamic is no longer important. We're no longer two separate entities jostling for prominence, and feeling inferior or superior according to our level of dominance. The boundaries between us fade away, as a flow of empathy unites us. Relationships no longer give us an ego-gratifying sense of status, but an infinitely more satisfying sense of communion and understanding.

Mindfulness

Another term for what I'm calling 'conscious attention' is mindfulness, of course. I've been using 'conscious attention' because it's more descriptive of the actual state. (I also think the term 'mindfulness' is potentially misleading, in that in everyday speech the 'mind' is usually equated with the intellect, which isn't involved in this state at all. In this sense, it could be more accurately called 'mind-emptiness.')

The great thing about using this as a practice is that, unlike sitting meditation, you can do it absolutely anywhere, in any situation. This is why some people find mindfulness more natural than sitting meditation, and why it's probably best to practice mindfulness first. Meditation and mindfulness – or conscious attention – are very similar, but the main difference between them is that in meditation we try to empty and still the mind, aiming to attain a state of pure (or at least purer) consciousness. Meditation is also usually done in *withdrawal* mode. It's something that you step out of your everyday life to do, when you go into a quiet room, sit down quietly and close your eyes. On the other hand, in mindfulness you don't try to do anything, you just observe what's happening around you. You don't try to quiet your mind; you just observe it. You don't withdraw from the world; you just give your whole attention to your experience *in* the world. You can eat, drink, walk, brush your teeth or talk to your friends mindfully, if you pay full attention to the activities, without analyzing them.

And eventually, as with the habit of positive thinking and dis-identifying from thoughts, at some point conscious attention will become so natural and habitual that you won't need to *practice* it anymore. You won't need to make a conscious effort to focus on the present; you will just *be* present.

Stage 7: Meditation

Meditation itself is a very necessary – and very effective – method of healing our minds too. In Chapter 9, we saw that meditation is the most effective way of temporarily transcending humania. Withdrawing from external stimuli and focusing our attention on a mantra (or our breathing or a candle flame) quiets our thought-chatter and softens the boundaries of the ego, so that we experience harmony of being. After a good practice these effects can last for hours.

But meditation has powerful *long-term* effects too. Over months or years of regular practice, it can help us to attain a state of permanent harmony.

The mistake made by many people is that they start meditating before they're ready. They enroll for meditation classes while there's still a lot of psychological discord inside them, before they've healed the effects of trauma, and before they've quieted their thought-chatter or dealt with underlying negative thought-patterns. If you meditate at this stage, it can be counterproductive, possibly even dangerous. You may find yourself engulfed by the pain of repressed traumatic experiences, or feel overwhelmed by the chaotic negativity of your thoughts. At the very least, you'll probably be scared off the practice for the foreseeable future. That's why it's so important to go through the previous six stages before sitting down to meditate. You need to have healed your psychological discord to a significant degree already. But by this point, particularly after practicing conscious attention, you should be able to adjust to sitting meditation fairly easily.

Meditation has been shown to have a massive array of benefits – physical benefits such as reduced blood pressure, a better immune system, and a greater resistance to pain; psychological benefits such as reduced anxiety and depression, and greater powers of concentration and attention.[2] It's also sometimes promoted as a way of coping with stress or enhancing your performance at work. In my view though, the main purpose – and the greatest benefit – of meditation is as a therapy for our disordered minds. It's the most effective way of healing and permanently transcending humania.

Research has shown that, like therapy, regular meditation causes physical changes to the brain. In a 2003 study, scientists at the University of Wisconsin scanned the brains of Buddhist monks who had been meditating for decades. They found that the monks' left prefrontal lobes – the areas of the brain linked with positive moods and emotions – were unusually active. Other studies of long-term meditators have shown that their cerebral cortex (the outer layer of the brain) was thicker in areas associated with attention and emotional integration.[3]

A 2011 study showed just how quickly these changes can occur. Sixteen people were given MRI brain scans before they took part in an eight-week program, which included weekly group meditations and guided audio meditations on CD every day. The participants meditated for an average of 27 minutes each day, and their brains were scanned again at the end of the eight weeks. The second scans showed increased 'gray matter' in parts of the brain associated with learning and memory, compassion and introspection. As for the Tibetan monks, there was also less gray matter – and less activity – in the amygdala, suggesting less anxiety and stress.[4]

Once again, this is good evidence of neuroplasticity. And for us, the really important point is that if meditation can bring about these neurological changes so quickly, it can certainly bring about *psychological* changes too. In the same way that it changes the physical structure and form of the brain, meditation can change the structure of the psyche – specifically, by permanently reducing our cognitive discord and by softening the boundaries of the ego.

This is part of the reason why it's so important to meditate regularly, and so allow the momentum of this change to build up. If you meditate twice a day for 20 minutes or more – and providing you have a reasonably good practice – each time you'll slightly weaken the normal structure of the psyche, in the same way that every gust of a strong wind gradually weakens the foundations of a fragile house. Although the normal structure will reestablish itself a few hours after you've meditated, it won't establish itself *quite* as strongly as before. It's a cumulative process – after a few months of regular meditation, you'll still be afflicted by thought-chatter, but it won't be quite as loud and chaotic as it was before. There will be a degree of inner stillness – or at least not as much inner disturbance – and you'll have some access to the reservoir of wellbeing that lies beneath the surface discontent of our minds. In addition, the sense of duality between you and your surroundings and between you and the activities you do will no longer be as strong. You'll begin to feel that you are part of the world rather than just an observer of it.

As I mentioned at the beginning of the last chapter, regular meditation will enhance the progress you've made at the earlier stages of this path. Going back to Stage 3, for example, meditation will help you to 'dis-identify' with your thoughts more, to stand apart from their flow rather than let them take you away. (As I mentioned in that section, the specific aim of *Vipassana* meditation is to detach ourselves from the stream of our thoughts and feelings, and just to witness and observe them.)

Similarly, with Stage 4, meditation will reduce the negative tone of your thinking. As your sense of ego-separateness and incompleteness fades away, the atmosphere of your mind will be less charged with anxiety. As a result, your thoughts will be less tinged with negativity, in the same way that a person's behavior will be less agitated and nervous in a large room filled with light rather than a small, dark room. Any leftover negative 'scripts' you have will become weaker, and hopefully disappear altogether.

And of course, meditation will help to further the progress you made at Stage 1, helping you to grow more used to your own mental space. After a few months of regular meditation, you should be well accustomed to the territory of your mind, and feel more at ease there. As a result, the impulse to immerse your attention in distractions and activities will die away even further.

This will also help you to *know yourself* in a way you never did before. Normally, because our attention is always focused externally, we're strangers to our own selves. All we know of our own selves is the surface level discord and discontent we try to run away from. But meditation enables us to go beneath the surface and explore our being more fully and deeply. It enables us to examine how our own minds work, how our thoughts and feelings arise, how external events affect our moods, and so on. It helps us to become more attuned to ourselves, to know when it's the right time to retreat and relax, or when it's time to be active. Unfamiliarity usually brings a degree of mistrust and fear, as with two neighbors who have lived next door to each other for years but have never spoken to each other. But once the neighbors start talking to each other and develop a relationship, the mistrust disappears. And it's the same with our inner being: once we begin to explore it and connect with it, fear is replaced by harmony.

Regular meditation may also give you a new sense of being *grounded* in yourself. When identity is rooted in the ego, it's always very changeable. Your feeling of who you are changes according to the mood you're in, the thoughts you're having, the roles you're playing and the people you're with. You may feel like a certain person when you're in a miserable mood at home alone, and another person when you're out enjoying yourself with your friends in the evening. You may have one identity when you're thinking about the past, and another when you think about the future. This may give you a frustrating sense of inconstancy, almost as if you're on a kind of identity carousel, which never stands still for more than a few hours. The esoteric philosopher G.I. Gurdjieff said that human beings consist of millions of different 'I's, constantly jostling to take over our consciousness. According to Gurdjieff, almost every second a new 'I' occupies the 'seat' of our identity, so that we have no genuine sense of self. This may be a slight exaggeration, but the essential idea is certainly valid.

However, meditation will make your sense of identity more stable. The millions of different 'I's will give way to a much more solid and deep-rooted 'I' that remains constant through all your different experiences and situations. There's a sense that this is who you *really* are – who you really were all the time; the essential self that was obscured like a blue sky behind clouds.

It's important to remember that, on a psychological level at least, there's nothing particularly esoteric about meditation. It's essentially just a way of quieting thought-chatter and softening the boundaries of the ego. As we saw in Chapter 9, there are a lot of other activities that have a similar effect, such as yoga, tai chi, swimming, and running, or contact with nature. All of these are 'meditative' activities to some degree, and I recommend doing one or more of them at the same time as practicing actual meditation, to intensify its effect. In particular, it's important to have regular contact with nature. As we saw earlier, contact with nature brings temporary experiences of harmony, precisely because of its meditative mind-quieting effect. In addition, nature helps to melt away our ego-boundaries, and reaffirms our sense that we're not isolated entities, but part of a vast and intricate web of life. So a daily quiet walk through the countryside – or through a park or nature reserve, if you live too far away from the countryside – will have a similar effect to meditation itself.

Stage 8: Healing the mind through quietness and stillness

Since harmony is the mind's most natural state, there is a natural tendency for us to return to it, in the same way that water returns to stillness without wind or waves. Under ego-madness, there is so much chaos in our minds that this tendency can't assert itself. You could compare this to our bodies: they have a natural tendency to return to a state of health, but if we're too busy and stressed, the process won't work. We have to give our body the *opportunity* to heal itself by resting and relaxing. And while our minds are full of chatter and busy taking in information and concentrating on tasks, the gravitational pull back to harmony is completely overridden. As with the body, we have to *allow* our minds to return to harmony.

At this point on the journey beyond humania, this natural tendency begins to aid us. As our minds become quieter, and as we learn to live inside ourselves, it begins to exert a subtle force that increases the momentum of our movement.

However, we also need to consciously *encourage* this tendency, by giving it as much opportunity as we can to manifest. And the primary way we can do this is to make space for quietness and stillness (or inactivity) in our lives. Quietness and stillness allow the pull toward harmony to assert itself, just as rest allows the body's healing properties to manifest.

For most people, quietness, stillness, and solitude are enemies to be avoided at all costs. Partly, again, this is a question of habituation. We live our lives against a backdrop of incessant noise – the chatter of TVs and radios, the roar of passing cars and airplanes, the clanging and whirring of machines. We're so accustomed to this background 'white noise' that when it ceases we feel uneasy. We're so used to the chattering of TVs and radios in our homes that when we come home to a silent house it feels wrong; the atmosphere seems somehow cold and empty.

But the main reason why we don't like quietness and solitude, of course, is because they expose us to our psychological discord. When we're alone we feel our ego-isolation, the seemingly unbridgeable gulf between ourselves and the world 'out there.' And silence means that there are no distractions around us to immerse our attention in, so that we experience the chaos and negativity of our thought-chatter.

However, once your psychological discord begins to heal, your attitude toward quietness and solitude will change radically. You will begin to relish them, rather than fear them. Rather than enemies, they will begin to seem like two of your greatest friends. Those empty moments of solitude that seemed painfully naked before will begin to seem comfortable and complete.

Whereas in our normal state silence and solitude expose us to the discord at the surface of our being, once that discord has faded away a little, they can bring us into contact with the harmony *beneath* the surface, the radiant wellbeing that fills the spacious expanse of our whole being. Whereas normally solitude makes us feel our *dis*connection from the world and other people, in this state it brings a profound experience of *connection* – to our own deeper selves, and to the world as a whole.

One person who experienced the healing power of quietness and solitude in a profound way is an Australian named Paul Narada Alister. In 1978, he was wrongly convicted of a terrorist attack and spent seven years in prison before being pardoned. In his book *Bombs, Bliss and Baba,* he describes how terrible life was for his fellow prisoners. Alone in the cells for several hours a day, the isolation made them aloof and mistrustful, and caused depression and suicidal tendencies. It also created a desperate need for distraction, leading to drug abuse, casual sex and gang activity. These are the effects of too much exposure to psychological discord that we've seen many times throughout this book. (Also recall Pascal's comment – in Chapter 1 – that it's this lack of diversion that makes prison such a fearful punishment.)

At first, Paul Narada Alister found the silence and solitude difficult to deal with too, but after a while he began to find it a blessing. He had already started to follow a spiritual way of life before prison, regularly meditating and doing yoga, which helped him to experience the positive side of silence and solitude. He used the time to reflect, contemplate and meditate for long periods, and started to experience a new sense of wellbeing and aliveness. He developed what he describes as 'a deep sense of freedom and positivity,' and found that he was able to function much better in his work at the prison and in his relationships with the other prisoners.

For these reasons he feels that he gained lasting benefits from his years in prison. As he writes:

> *The inner silence that prison afforded me gave me an experience I carry to this day. I no longer avoid solitude or isolation. If anything I look forward to [them] as a time to experience that inner silence which can give me so much bliss. Be it in meditation or just enjoying my own company, I find silence is golden when experienced as a way to get in touch with my spiritual self.*[5]

The novelist Sara Maitland had a similar experience when she spent six weeks in silence and solitude in a remote cottage on the Isle of Skye in the Scottish Highlands. The first thing she was aware of was a heightening of perception. As she describes it, 'By the end of the second week I was feeling everything with an extraordinary degree of intensity.'[6] Later she began to experience a strong sense of oneness with her surroundings that she describes as 'a connection as though my skin had been blown off... I felt absolutely connected to everything.' And these experiences were underpinned by a growing sense of wellbeing: 'Moments of intense happiness, followed by a powerful conviction that the moment was somehow a pure gift.'[7]

The important factor here is that both Paul Narada Alister and Sara Maitland had already transcended ego-madness to some degree. The difference between Paul and his fellow prisoners was that his meditation practice (and his spiritual way of life before prison) meant that there was less psychological discord inside him, which enabled him to embrace silence and solitude. Similarly, Sara Maitland is a devout Catholic, accustomed to prayer and contemplation. For someone with a normal degree of psychological discord, six weeks of silence and solitude would probably lead to breakdown or insanity. But for her – as for Paul – far from giving rise to discontent and unease, they had a powerful positive effect, helping her mind to return to a natural state of harmony.

What I'm suggesting, then, is that you should make a conscious effort to bring quietness into your life, thinking of it as a kind of spiritual practice, akin to meditation or yoga. Perhaps give yourself two or three evenings each week – or perhaps one whole day – to spend in silence, doing very little. Think of these as your 'retreat' times. Unplug the TV, computer and CD player and enjoy the warm, spacious silence that fills the room. You don't need to spend the whole evening or day doing nothing – you could do a few jobs around the house or a little reading. In fact, doing these activities against a background of stillness will help ensure that you do them with conscious attention.

Quietness doesn't necessarily mean solitude either. You may want to spend the evening quietly with your partner, or with a good friend. If you're both comfortable with silence, you won't need to talk a great deal. In fact, if you spend time with another person against a background of comfortable silence, you'll find that you're able to communicate more fully and intimately, even though you might talk much less. Rather than dividing your attention between your companion and some music or the radio or TV, you give your whole self to them. You experience the power and presence of their being as well as of your own, and if your relationship with them has any discord, that will fade away too, like your own psychological discord.

But it's important to spend some time in solitude too. Remember that having contact with your own self is just as important as contact with other people. Your relationship with your deeper being has to be nurtured just as friendships do, and it's easier to do this in solitude rather than in company.

It's completely natural to have friends and to socialize, and some of the most powerful and profound experiences of our lives can come through contact with other people. I'm certainly not saying that we should completely withdraw from society and become hermits in the desert. But in humania, our *natural* need for social contact is exaggerated by our psychological discord. As with other activities, we often use social activity as a way of escaping from our selves. We talk to try to divert our attention from our psychological discord, covering up our thought-chatter with real verbal chatter. (We prefer real verbal chatter to thought-chatter because we have some control over it, and it doesn't take place inside our heads and so doesn't reinforce our sense of ego-isolation.) Conversations immerse our attention in the same way that TV shows and books do, and so help us to avoid experiencing our inner discord.

On the other hand, our basic state of ego-isolation and incompleteness *impels* us to make contact with other people. We need social contact to try to soften the essential loneliness we feel, to try to bridge the gulf we experience between the inner and outer. Social contact can genuinely help us in this way, when we have meaningful and intimate contact with another person and the boundary between our self and theirs melts away. All too often though, we talk to other people without really making connection with them. Socializing often doesn't really soften the isolation we feel, just distract us from it.

However, once you begin to move toward harmony, you won't be psychologically dependent on social contact. You won't need to frantically phone around friends if you see a sequence of empty evenings in front of you – instead, you'll look forward to spending the time quietly and sedately with yourself. You might find that you have fewer friends than before, but these friendships will be more intimate and genuine. You'll enjoy solitude and at the same time relish communication and friendship when you have them. As with solitude itself, you'll have a different attitude to social contact. You won't think of it as a source of fun or distraction, but as a source of empathy and connection, a way of melting boundaries and sharing goodwill.

This is, of course, why silence and solitude are integral parts of the monastic way of life. For monks, silence is a spiritual practice. Most monasteries have silent places, such as the church, refectory or dormitory, and certain times – including the nighttime – when speaking is strictly prohibited. Silence is seen as a way of developing self-knowledge and of clearing the mind of distractions, and so leaving it open to God. (Some monastic orders even use forms of sign language to help them to preserve silence.) Most monks live in communities, but still designate certain periods of the day for solitary prayer, reading or reflection. Admittedly, some monastic traditions seem to take this to an unhealthy extreme – for example, Carthusian monks spend all day alone in their cells, apart from three daily visits to the church. (They're also only allowed to speak to each other twice a week, once on Sundays after lunch, and once on Mondays during a communal walk.) But at the heart of these practices is the recognition that silence and stillness are gateways to inner peace.

Living slowly and simply

Although it manifests itself most powerfully through silence and solitude, the gravitational pull of harmony can also express itself in the active part of our lives. Normally, the complexity and busy-ness of our lives overloads our minds, bombarding us with information and fuelling a whirlwind of thought, so that the gravitational pull of harmony can't act. And nothing is more opposed to a state of harmony than the act of rushing, when our minds are overloaded with demands and completely ignore the present in an effort to reach the future as quickly as possible. But if we can reduce the general complexity and busy-ness of our lives, and make a conscious effort to live *slowly* and simply, then it's possible that, even in our active phases, there will be enough stillness inside us for the gravitational pull of harmony to express itself.

Again, you'll find yourself doing this naturally as you move toward harmony, but it's also something that you can work on consciously. It simply means making sure that your life isn't too cluttered with demands and activities. On a practical level, it could mean reducing your working hours (if you can afford it) and unloading unnecessary possessions. We sometimes forget that possessions are a burden, and take up our energy and attention. The more we have, the more time we spend looking after them and the more they drain our energy away. We don't own them; they own us. Living simply could also mean reducing your obligations to other people, such as the number of e-mail correspondents you keep in contact with or the number of organizations you're involved with.

It's also worth making a conscious effort to live slowly, and to try to avoid rushing whenever possible. Whenever you become aware of yourself rushing – when you're cooking, eating, walking, cleaning your house, working or talking to someone – just stop for a second to reorientate yourself in the present. Make a conscious effort to do the activity slowly instead. Don't rush eating your meal – resist the pull of the future and take your time. Relish the taste of the food instead of unconsciously chewing and swallowing. Don't rush when you're driving – focus your thoughts away from your destination, and don't think of this journey as just an irritating inconvenience to be eliminated as quickly as possible. Slow down and bring your attention to the act of driving and to the buildings and streets around you. Remember that it doesn't matter if you're a couple of minutes late – it's more important to cultivate a calm state of mind rather than to arrive stressed with a mind full of thought-chatter.

As the example of driving shows, slowing down is closely connected to conscious attention, as in Stage 6. They facilitate each other. Slowing down *allows* us to give conscious attention to what we're doing; and bringing conscious attention to what we're doing naturally slows us down. It's impossible to practice conscious attention when we hurry.

To summarize then, I recommend these eight stages as a way of healing humania and attaining a state of permanent harmony of being:

1. Learn the habit of resting inside your own mental space, reducing your dependency on distractions and activities.
2. If it's difficult for you to face your psychological discord due to the effects of trauma, seek help to try to heal this.
3. Learn to step back and 'dis-identify' with your thought-chatter, observing it rather than being carried along.
4. Change the negative tone of your thoughts, by identifying your underlying negative scripts and challenging and replacing them, using the type of cognitive exercises described above.
5. Practice some form of service.
6. Practice 'conscious attention' or mindfulness during your daily life.
7. Mediate at least once a day for 20 to 30 minutes, and/or practice other 'meditative' activities such as contact with nature, running, or swimming
8. Make a conscious effort to take 'retreat' periods of quietness and stillness, as well as to live simply and slowly.

CHAPTER 12

A New Self and a New World

In humania we only skim the surface of life. Many of us go through decades of our lives continuously flitting from one distraction or activity to the next, with just the occasional period of uneasy introspection in-between. We live in a kind of trance, alienated from our true selves and from the real world. Sometimes in middle age we may shake ourselves out of the trance for a few moments, in times of existential crisis when we suddenly look at our lives and wonder, 'Where am I? How did I get here? What have I been doing for the last 20 years?'

In harmony, we wake up out of this trance permanently, and it's only then that we truly begin to live. It's only then that we become truly *worthy* of life. While we suffer from humania, we *escape* from life, rather than actually live.

Living in a state of harmony changes us in so many ways that it's almost impossible to describe them all. One of the most immediate effects of healing ego-madness is a sense of liberation, now that we're free of the constant atmosphere of anxiety inside our minds. That oppressive atmosphere lifts, like a band of heavy cloud dispersing, and we realize that *there is nothing to worry about.* We're so used to that constant underlying anxiety that we don't even realize it's there. But when it fades away it leaves a state of ease that feels completely natural and right.

We also feel liberated because we're free of the continual *pressure* that our normal psychological discord creates, pushing us outside ourselves and forcing us to look for new places to immerse our attention. In our normal state we're like drug addicts, with a constant nagging need inside us, trying to feed ourselves with a continual supply of activities and distractions. But in harmony, this pressure disappears, and we feel lighter and more peaceful and free. We're free of the pressure *to do.* Activity and distraction are no longer necessary, in the same way that painkillers are no longer necessary once a wound has healed. We're able to face the present completely nakedly, and rather than being uncomfortable, it's wonderfully warm and benevolent. Like recovered drug addicts, freed from the constant internal pressure to *seek* something, we feel a sense of lightness, as if a massive burden has been lifted.

In our culture the term 'doing nothing' has powerful negative connotations. In a world that never comes to rest, 'doing nothing' is seen as lazy and unproductive. But to truly 'do nothing' is a very rare ability. People sometimes say that they've 'done nothing' over the weekend or during a week off work. But on closer inspection, they really just mean that they've just not engaged in any activities that our society considers productive. It means that they've been lying in bed, watching TV, reading magazines, doing puzzles, chatting to friends on the phone, rather than working, doing DIY or traveling to different places. They haven't really been doing nothing since they've still had their minds occupied with activities and distractions. *Really* doing nothing is infinitely harder than this, and doesn't imply any laziness or passivity. On the contrary, truly doing nothing means being alive to the present moment and to your own self, alert to every experience and sensation. It means being able to truly *relax,* without the feeling that there are activities or duties to attend to and complete. And it only becomes possible to do this in a state of harmony. It's only then that you truly become a human *being.*

In the exact reverse of our normal anxious state (where we feel anxious even when there's nothing tangible to be anxious *about*), in a state of harmony you find yourself feeling happy even when there's nothing tangible to be happy about. We're so used to associating happiness with external things – good news or good fortune, enjoyable activities or praise or compliments – that sometimes you might become aware of this inner wellbeing and say to yourself, 'That's strange – I wonder why I'm feeling so happy? What good things have happened to me recently?' But nothing has happened. This happiness doesn't have an external source. It's not even just the absence of *un*happiness. It's a happiness that is the essence of our being, or, more specifically, the quality of the energy that constitutes our being.

Once you've made contact with this natural source of wellbeing, there's no need to look for happiness outside you. You don't have to chase after money and success, or seek hedonistic thrills from drink, drugs, fast cars, wild nights out or shopping. (This is another way in which we feel liberated – because we're free of the *desire* for these things.) The irony is that we're conditioned into thinking of happiness as something that we have to reach out and *get* from the world. But really happiness is an *inner* condition. We're like people who have heard that a hoard of treasure is buried somewhere and scour the whole world in search of it. They never find it, because all the time it was right under their noses, buried in their own backyards. Happiness is so close to us that we can't see it. In harmony, we realize that it doesn't come from what we do or what we have, but from *being*.

In humania, our being is like a forest whose perimeter is dark, overgrown and dangerous. When we go into it we feel anxious and so try to spend all our time outside it. But the perimeter is deceptive. Because it's so thick – and because our anxiety makes us reluctant to go any further – we rarely go beyond it. But sometimes, in the right state of mind, the darkness and danger fade away, and the foliage thins out enough to allow us through, into the heart of the forest. There it's light and spacious, with a clearing between the trees, and we become aware of how beautiful and benevolent the forest really is.

And in a permanent state of harmony, the darkness and danger disappear completely. The forest no longer has a perimeter. As soon as you enter it, you're in its warm and peaceful core.

And since we no longer need to escape from ourselves, we're no longer pushed away from the *present* either. The future and the past no longer have as much meaning to us. The present is our home, and we only go elsewhere when we need to – perhaps to make plans and to learn from past mistakes. We do everything we need to do slowly and mindfully, without being dragged toward the end of the activity – and toward the next one – by our impatience. We step off the train of linear time, and stop in the present. It feels like finally coming to rest after hours or days in constant motion.

In humania, life is always a struggle – a struggle to turn our attention away from our psychological discord, our fundamental isolation and incompleteness, and the disturbance inside us; a constant battle to keep ourselves busy and find new ways of distracting ourselves, or to compensate for our inner discontent or bolster our fragile egos. But in harmony life becomes easy. There is no more struggle. There is no need for activity or distraction, no need to look forward to the future or to rush, no need to get drunk or take drugs, no need for wealth or power.

There is no need for any of these things because there is *no need*. Need is an expression of lack. In harmony there is no lack. The present is always enough. We accept it on its own terms; we don't need to escape from it or to try to complete it. It's always complete in itself. Far from being empty, it's always full of beauty and benevolence.

Beyond separation

We've seen that a lot of the suffering and pathological behavior that fills our lives is caused by our ego-separation. And in the same way, transcending this separation affects our behavior positively. In a state of harmony, the self is no longer an isolated and incomplete entity. We're no longer trapped inside our heads with the world 'out there' on the other side. The boundary has faded away. We have become part of the cosmos, rather than broken fragments of it. We have become participants rather than observers, part of the smooth flow of shared experience.

As a result, we no longer need to bolster the fragile ego with psychological attachments like possessions. We don't need to believe in anything, to hope for anything, to possess anything, or to uphold an image of ourselves as good-looking, successful, knowledgeable, or powerful. You might still *have* knowledge or success – or even possessions – but you don't depend on them for your wellbeing. It wouldn't matter very much if they disappeared. We don't need to attach ourselves to anything, because we feel self-sufficient and complete.

For the same reason, we no longer need group identity. We don't need to join gangs, support football teams, or follow fashions. We don't need to tie up our identity with a religion, or an ethnic or social group, and feel that our group is distinct and superior to other groups. You might still follow the customs and practices of a cultural or religious tradition, just because they're closest to you, at the same time as being aware that religions and cultures are like vegetation – they just develop in a different way in different parts of the world, without any inherent superiority. You don't feel that your group are 'the chosen ones,' that you possess the truth, or feel an impulse to spread your traditions to others. You know that any differences between human beings are just incidental and superficial. You feel a deep connection to other people that transcends culture or religion.

The loss of separateness also means that our fear of death decreases. Now that we feel a sense of connection – to other people, nature, and the whole universe itself – we no longer feel that the end of our individual existence is such a devastating tragedy. We no longer feel so attached to our past achievements, our future ambitions, our possessions and relationships. As a result, we feel able to let go of them. We know that we're not the center of the universe, and that the world will exist perfectly well without us. (By this point we may well have developed a sense that death is not the end of our existence anyway, that the deepest core of our being may survive the death of the body, and become a part of the cosmos.)

Our relationships are also transformed by this lack of separateness. It opens us up to other people, brings us into empathic connection with them, so that we feel a strong identification with them, and a desire to help them. Because we're bonded to them, we can feel their frustration and sorrow, their joy, and relief. Our own desires are no longer so important to us. What *is* important is to try to alleviate other people's suffering and further their development. Other people are no longer just competitors for wealth and status, no longer adversaries who we judge and deride to make us feel better about ourselves. They're no longer foreign beings who we feel threatened by, and whose approval we seek. The connection we feel toward them dissolves away discord and mistrust. How can hostility exist when there's no separation?

This also means that we can communicate deeply and fully with other people. When you're with another person, the two of you are no longer just two isolated egos communicating superficially across a great gulf, second-guessing each other's thoughts and feelings, and afraid of revealing your true selves. The deep flow of empathy and energy between you enables you to truly *know* each other. You reach beneath the surface ego to each other's true self, just as you make contact with your own deeper self. And as a result, there's a bond of deep understanding and trust.

A new vision of reality

Once our inner world has changed, the outer world changes too. In harmony, the world becomes a completely different place. Our eyes are opened wider, with fuller and brighter vision, so that we can perceive a new world of is-ness and meaning. We realize that we made a mistake in assuming that our old normal vision of the world was objective and true.

In our normal state, we see our surroundings through a fog of thought-chatter, giving them very little attention. As a result, they often appear dreary and one-dimensional. Trees, flowers, animals, rivers, the sky, and the buildings around us seem so mundane that they hardly seem worth looking at. We perceive them as objects, with no being of their own, and no connection to each other. But in a state of harmony, we become aware of an underlying beauty and meaning. We realize that the world isn't inanimate or indifferent. Trees, rivers, stones, and clouds and even man-made buildings are more distinct and beautiful – and *alive.* An energy seems to flow through them and to radiate from them, *making* them alive. We realize that our old vision of the world was limited and deceptive, like a blurred picture from an old video camera compared to a new high-definition one.

The 'meaning of life' isn't something that can be formulated or put into words. It's something that is just *there,* a real, tangible atmosphere that we can either sense or not sense. You can feel it around you, as a benevolent energy. This meaning makes us aware that it's somehow *right* for us to be here at this moment on this surface of the planet. It makes us feel 'at home' in the world.

In harmony, we also come to truly *know* the world, in the same way that we come to truly know ourselves. In humania, the world is a foreign place, just like our own being. Our surroundings are an incidental backdrop that we pay little or no attention to, like a painting on your living-room wall that you haven't truly looked at for years. In fact, we can't really know the world because we don't live *in* it.

But in harmony, we become true inhabitants of this planet, and we see it in all its intricacy and is-ness, its depths of wonder and beauty.

Harmony and activity

Once humania has been healed, you'll certainly find that you become less active, because you've lost the compulsion to be busy. Now you'll only do things out of interest, enjoyment, altruism and practical necessity, rather than out of the *psychological* necessity to escape your own mind-space. At the same time, you'll find that you become much more efficient and effective in your activities. In humania, when you try to focus on an activity, there's thought-chatter flowing through your mind, competing for your attention and interrupting your concentration. For example, you could be working on a computer program, filling in forms or writing a novel, but every so often you find that your mind drifts off, and you're busy thinking about the beautiful woman or man you saw at a bar last night, or about the food you need to buy for a dinner party you're having later.

But in harmony, when thought-chatter becomes quieter, the beam of your attention is much stronger and steadier. It isn't interrupted by thought-chatter, and so you don't have to keep dragging it back to its object like a reluctant child. Your concentration becomes more effortless and natural, and you accomplish more with less energy. You do what you have to do, and then move on.

In a similar way, harmony also enables us to *think* more clearly. It doesn't necessarily mean stopping thinking altogether. We become free of automatic involuntary thinking, but we're still able to think *consciously* if we need to. That is, we're still able to make decisions and plans and to think logically in order to solve problems. As I said in Chapter 2, thought-chatter makes it difficult for us to think in a rational, conscious way, because it tends to take over our attention, and makes it difficult for us to focus on the matter at hand. It's like trying to walk in a straight line along a crowded street. First of all you need to find a starting point among all the chaos of spinning thoughts, and even when you've started walking, new thoughts keep arising and trying to take you off in different directions. It can also lead to associations that prejudice our judgment – for example, you might have to make a decision about whether to give someone a job, but you notice that his name is 'Jones,' which reminds you of another person called Jones you used to work with who you didn't get on with, which subconsciously turns you against this person called Jones...

But now that our minds are free – or at least more free – of thought-chatter, our 'conscious thinking' becomes clearer and more effective. To continue the metaphor above, the street is clear so it's easy to walk in a straight line.

New energy

Another positive effect of harmony of being is how much *energy* it gives us.

Humania has a powerful energy-draining effect. On the one hand, filling our lives with activity to keep our attention focused outside ourselves uses up a massive amount of energy. I'm not talking so much about *physical* muscular energy, but about the *mental* energy we expend when we concentrate, communicate and process information. We perform these mental functions almost constantly throughout our days, when we work, socialize, write e-mails, make phone calls, surf the Internet, play games and so on. We're constantly concentrating or processing information, so there's a constant outflow of energy.

Living your life against a background of noise and movement also has an energy-draining effect too. In the modern world – especially in towns and cities – we're bombarded with a massive amount of external stimuli. Our fields of vision are crowded with constantly shifting objects, while our ears are bombarded with a cacophony of different sounds. Our minds edit out the most familiar stimuli, but there's still a massive amount of information for us to process, and we use up a lot of energy in doing so. Think about how you feel after a trip into the city center on a busy shopping day, for instance – you arrive home and feel like collapsing onto your sofa for half an hour, and this isn't so much because of the walking you've been doing, but because of the mental energy you've used up processing the urban noise around you and the chaos of moving crowds and cars.

The activity *inside* us is a problem too. Our thought-chatter also has an energy-draining effect. We don't normally consider the idea that thinking expends energy, but it's also an activity, and is 'fuelled' by mental energy in the same way that a radio is fuelled by electricity. And so if your mind is very busy, and there's a constant stream of wild thought-material spinning through your mind, this will use up a significant amount of energy too.

In fact, in the modern world our lives are so full of activity and external stimuli, and our minds are so full of thought-chatter that many of us live in a state of chronic 'energy-shortage,' which can lead to health problems. To stay healthy we have to allow our energies to regenerate, which requires relaxation. But many of us don't allow ourselves to relax properly. In humania, it's difficult to do this, because true relaxation means being free of activity and distractions, which means turning inward and experiencing our psychological discord. Often the only kind of relaxation we experience is when we stop being busy and only expose ourselves to the least energy-intensive distractions, like TV. But this still involves some concentration and information processing, and so isn't complete relaxation.

Sometimes our bodies seem to forcibly remove us from activity and stimuli for a while by making us ill, so that we have no choice but to do nothing and allow our energies to regenerate. But some people can carry on 'running on empty' for a long time, living off the adrenaline of constant activity – which might seem attractive in the short term, but will ultimately lead to serious health problems.

But in harmony of being this problem disappears. Since you're less active and have more silence and solitude in your life, you expend much less energy through concentration and processing information. Since your mind is quieter you expend much less energy in thinking. And just as importantly, in a state of harmony you're able to relax *properly*. It's no problem at all for you to withdraw from activity and external stimuli for a while and allow your mental energy to regenerate

– in fact it's a pleasure to do this. And so you never suffer from a shortage of energy. On the contrary, there's always a *surplus* of energy inside you, a dynamo of vitality that means that you rarely get tired and are always full of enthusiasm and *joie de vivre*. And as an added bonus, this will improve your health.

A new world

More important than how it affects us as individuals, however, is how a state of harmony affects us – or *could* affect us, if enough people in the world could experience it – collectively, as a species.

The end point of humania is global chaos and destruction. Ever since its emergence, humania has been moving toward catastrophe. This catastrophe is already underway – more and more natural disasters caused by environmental change, dwindling water supplies, the death of millions of species, coupled with a bizarre indifference to – and even denial of – our predicament. How could it be any other way? An insane species can't survive indefinitely on a fragile and finite planet. Billions of people with infinite desires and an infinite capacity for conflict and brutality – and no sense of connection to the network of nature they are intimately bound up with – are destined to self-destruct eventually. A species that can't live with itself is bound to destroy itself.

Our only real hope for survival as a species is therefore to transcend humania. Transcending humania also means transcending the pathological behavior the condition gives rise to. While we suffer from ego-separateness and cognitive discord, these pathologies will always exist, even though we might be able to control or mitigate them to some degree.

There will always be warfare, inequality, oppression and environmental destruction. There will always be dogmatic religions, and there will always be sharply defined ethnic or religious groups in conflict with each other. Ultimately, all discord in the world stems from the discord inside us.

But once our minds are healed, we no longer contribute to these pathologies. Since we feel whole inside, there's no need to try to complete ourselves with wealth and status. Since we feel a deep-rooted natural contentment, there's no need for us to try to compensate for dissatisfaction by trying to become significant and powerful or chasing after the hedonistic thrills of shopping and consuming. Now that we have learned the ability to *be,* it's no longer important for us to *have.*

In a similar way, we no longer need to strengthen our fragile egos by identifying with a religion, nationality or ideology, and thinking of any different groups as 'the other.' We no longer think of these other groups as inferior and withhold our empathy and respect from them. Instead, we feel a natural sense of empathy with them, a sense of connection and compassion that transcends superficial differences. Rather than feeling any desire to exploit or oppress them, we feel a desire to connect with them, to support and help them and reduce their suffering. And this sense of empathy extends to nature too. We feel a strong sense of connection to it, together with a sense of responsibility. Our heightened perception means that we can sense its *aliveness* too, rather than seeing it as just an inanimate supply of resources – and so we treat it with much more respect.

If a large enough number of people could transcend humania, the world would be a vastly different place. War and conflict would massively decrease, if not disappear altogether. The oppression of women, other ethnic groups or classes, and castes would decrease. Religious and ethnic differences would be seen as insignificant and fade away. Our suicidal destruction of the environment would be reigned in, and eventually cease.

This sounds absurdly utopian, of course, because we're so far away from this state at the moment. We're so close to self-destruction already, and humania holds such sway over us as a species, that we may never reach this point at all. But in the past, utopias have always failed because they haven't taken account of the reality of human nature. Communism failed because it didn't take into account the drive to accumulate wealth and status generated by humania. (Even when communism existed in name, it was distorted by self-interest and status-seeking, so that supposedly communist states became riddled with inequality and hierarchy too.) Most political and religious communes have failed for similar reasons, driven apart by conflicts over power, status, sex and possessions.

But a utopia isn't unrealistic if it stems from inner change. To a large extent, human society is always a reflection of human nature. And it's important to remember that human nature isn't fixed. It's no longer possible to believe – as many Neo-Darwinists and evolutionary psychologists do – that we're all just helplessly acting out behavioral traits that our ancestors developed on the African savannahs hundreds of thousands of years ago. The brain and the psyche are pliable, and we can make a conscious effort to change them.

Once we begin to transcend humania as individuals, we'll be making it easier for others to do the same. Over the last few decades, in some parts of the world – such as Western Europe – there has been a significant decrease in social identity and 'otherness,' which helps to explain why many European countries have not been at war with each other for nearly 70 years. An increased sense of empathy seems to have developed, which has led to increasing respect for the rights of others, and better treatment for groups who were once brutalized and marginalized, such as gays, people with disabilities, or ethnic minorities. (This also extends across species, with an increasing empathy for animals, leading to practices like vegetarianism and the animal rights movement.) There has also been a movement toward reconnection with nature, exemplified by the green movement, together with an increasing respect for the cultures and the wisdom of indigenous peoples. And just as significantly, there has been massive upsurge of interest in self-development and spirituality.

All of these developments suggest a movement beyond the separation and selfishness of humania. They suggest that the momentum for a collective psychological change – a transcendence of ego-madness – is building up. Perhaps at some point we'll reach a critical threshold where the psychological 'mold' of humania will fade away, so that it will no longer become our 'normal' state as we move into adulthood.

So with every step you move beyond ego-madness yourself, you may be helping to create a new world, helping to dispel the dark shadow that has been hanging over the human psyche for thousands of years. You may be helping to usher in a new spirit of collective harmony.

Ultimately, we can only transcend conflict in the world by healing it in our own being. We can only create peace in the world by creating peace in ourselves. As the Lakota Indian Black Elk said:

> *The first peace, which is the most important, is that which comes within the souls of people when they realize their relationship, their oneness with the universe and all its powers, and when they realize that at the center of the universe dwells the Great Spirit, and that its center is really everywhere, it is within each of us.*[1]

When we transcend humania, life ceases to be painful and dissatisfying, and becomes a glorious adventure, full of joy and wonder. After years of incompleteness, we become whole. After years of being asleep, we wake up. After years of escaping from the present, the world, and our own selves, we now rest comfortably within them.

After thousands of years of anxiety and confusion, wandering through a hostile world like refugees, we are finally home.

Notes

Introduction

1. Jung, 2002, p.42
2. In Wright, 1992, p.304
3. Chief Luther Standing Bear, 2011
4. 'Global Issues,' 2011
5. *The Diagnostic and Statistical Manual of Mental Disorders IV-TR*, 2000, p. xxxi

Part I: The Madness of Human Beings

Chapter 1: The Madness of Living Outside Ourselves

1. Solomon et al., 2004, p.129
2. Argyle, 1989; Raphael, 1984
3. Pascal, 1966, p.68
4. Ibid.

Chapter 2: Psychological Discord

1. Geertz, 1973; Gardiner et al., 1998
2. Ravuvu, 1983, p.7
3. Markus & Kitayama, 1991

4. Scott, 1997; Lawlor, 1991
5. Coleridge, 2011
6. Killingsworth, M. A., & Gilbert, 2010
7. Meister Eckhart, 1996, p.52
8. There is, however, some doubt about the long-term efficacy of CBT (e.g. Westen et al., 2004)
9. Krippner, 1999, p.64

Chapter 3: The Subtle Effects of Humania

1. Lawrence, 1994, p.610
2. Rudgley, 1993
3. Kosten et al., 2000
4. Stewart, 1996

Chapter 4: The Madness of Elsewhereness

1. Pascal, 1966, p.43

Chapter 5: The Madness of Constant Wanting

1. In Wright, 1992, p.361
2. Josephy, 1975
3. Kasser, 2002; Kasser et al., 2004
4. Seligman, 2011; Compton & Hoffman, 2012
5. Csikszentmihalyi, 1994
6. Cossey, 2011

Chapter 6: Collective Madness

1. Ehrenreich, 1996
2. Turner, 1994
3. 'Global Issues,' 2011
4. El-Zanaty et al., 1996

5. Goldberg, 1973
6. Amnesty International document – 'Pakistan: Honour killings of women and girls,' 2011
7. Wareing, 1999
8. Baron-Cohen, 2003, p.52
9. Ibid, 2003
10. Chief Seattle, 2011
11. In Swain, 1992, p.134
12. Chief Luther Standing Bear, 2011
13. Chief Edward Moody, 2011

Chapter 7: The Fragile Self

1. Daly & Wilson, 1983
2. Castaneda & Klein, 2011
3. Institute of Alcohol Studies, 2011
4. Lacan, 1977
5. 'Adolf Hitler's maid says Nazi was charming to work for,' 2011
6. Jaishankar & Haldar, 2011
7. Chief Red Jacket, 2011

Chapter 8: The Origins of Humania

1. Sahlins, 1972
2. Lawlor, R., 1991
3. Miracle & Dios, 1981
4. Hall, 1984
5. Kropotkin, 2006, p.91
6. Turnbull, 1993, p.29
7. Everett, 2008, p.85
8. Csikszentmihalyi, 1992, p.228
9. Woodburn, 1982, p.432

10. Woodburn, 2005, p.21
11. Boehm, 1999
12. Ingold et al., 1988
13. For example, in his TED talk 'On the myth of violence' – and also in his recent book *The Better Angels of our Nature* (2011) – Steven Pinker claims that men in hunter–gatherer societies were more likely to die a violent death than men alive today. He bases this on data from seven hunter–gatherer societies, none of which are representative. For a start, none of them are 'immediate-return' societies, as human beings were for 95 percent of our time on this planet. Three of his groups are from the Amazon, a region where indigenous groups have always been known to be much more violent and warlike than normal (due to a combination of historical and geographical factors). Another of the groups he chooses are the Murngin of northern Australia, who had suffered massive cultural disruption by the time data was collected in 1975. There are similar issues with the other three groups. (See Ryan and Jetha, 2010, for a fuller discussion.)
14. van der Dennen, 1995
15. Wildman, 1996
16. Lawlor, 1991
17. Jung, 2002, p.42
18. Josephy, 1975; Cocker, 1998

Part II: The Return to Harmony and Sanity

Chapter 9: Experiences of Harmony of Being

1. In Brown, 2004, p.viii
2. Byrd, 1987, p.144
3. Pretty *et al.*, 2007
4. Csikszentmihalyi, 1992, p.53
5. Ibid., pp.58–9
6. Dillard, 1974, p.197
7. Incidentally, readers of my earlier book, *Waking From Sleep*, may wonder how these states of 'harmony of being' relate to the 'awakening experiences' I refer to in that book.

   Essentially, they are the same experience. The difference is really just one of emphasis. In states of harmony of being, the emphasis is on the *inner* aspect, the sense of wholeness and wellbeing we feel inside; while in awakening experiences the emphasis is on the *outer* aspect, how our perception and our relationship to the world changes. The 'awakening' in awakening experiences is mainly one of vision, of perceiving new reality, beauty and meaning in the world, of perceiving the underlying unity of seeming separate things. The harmony in experiences of 'harmony of being' is that of being free of cognitive discord and ego-separateness: an experience of inner stillness and fullness. But in the vast majority of cases, an awakening experience is also an experience of harmony of being, and an experience of harmony of being is also an awakening experience. The sense of inner wellbeing always goes together with the change in perception.

There is just one exception to this. In *Waking From Sleep,* I suggest that there are two different types of awakening experiences. First of all, there are experiences caused by a disruption of the normal functioning of the brain and the body. I call these states of 'homeostasis-disruption' (or HD states), which can be generated by fasting, sleep deprivation, self-inflicted pain, breathing exercises, psychedelic drugs, and so on. Secondly, there are awakening experiences that occur when our inner energy – the energy of our being, or our 'life-energy' – becomes intensified and stilled. (I call these 'ISLE' states, standing for 'intensification and stilling of life-energy.') This can happen through meditation, sports, sex, contact with nature, and so on. One important difference between these two types of awakening experiences is that states of 'homeostasis-disruption' are usually not experiences of harmony of being. They usually don't bring inner stillness and a serene sense of wellbeing. There is usually still some mental chatter, which can be amplified and distorted into hallucinations or delusions. There may be a sense of wellbeing in HD states, but it's usually a wilder, more excitable and unstable kind – a 'high arousal' state of ecstasy or exhilaration rather than serenity or inner peace. But ISLE states are also an experience of harmony of being.

Chapter 10: Going Inside

1. Draganski *et al.*, 2006
2. Schwarz *et al.*, 2005
3. Radhu *et al.*, 2011
4. Lichter *et al.*, 1980
5. Wood *et al.*, 2009
6. Lally *et al.*, 2010

Chapter 11: Cultivating Inner Harmony

1. Jones, 2004, p.362
2. Andresen, 2000
3. Davidson *et al.*, 2003
4. Hölzel *et al.*, 2011
5. Alister, 1997, p.171
6. Maitland, 2010, p.48
7. Ibid., p.63

Chapter 12: A New Self and A New World

1. Black Elk, 2011

Bibliography

'**Adolf** Hitler's maid says Nazi was charming to work for' (2011). *The Telegraph*, 4/12/2008.
Retrieved 6/8/11 from http://www.telegraph.co.uk/news/worldnews/europe/germany/3547047/Adolf-Hitlers-maid-says-Nazi-was-charming-to-work-for.html

Alister, P. N. (1997). *Bombs, Bliss and Baba.* Maleny, Qld: Better World Books.

Amnesty International. (2011). 'Document - Pakistan: Honour killings of women and girls.' Retrieved 13/9/11 from http://www.amnesty.org/en/library/asset/ASA33/018/1999/en/952457dd-e0f1-11dd-be39-2d4003be4450/asa330181999en.html

Andresen, J. (2000). 'Meditation Meets Behavioural Medicine.' *The Journal of Consciousness Studies,* 7, 11–12, pp.17–73.

Argyle, M. (1989). *The Social Psychology of Work.* (2nd Edition). London: Penguin.

Baron-Cohen, S. (2003). *The Essential Difference: Men, Women and the Extreme Male Brain.* London: Allen Lane.

Black Elk. (2011). 'The First Peace.' Retrieved 3/7/2011 from http://www.firstpeople.us/FP-Html-Wisdom/BlackElk.html

Boehm, C. (1999). *Hierarchy in the Forest.* Cambridge, MA: Harvard University Press.

Brown, N. (2004). 'Introduction.' In *Air fare: Stories, Poems*

& *Essays on Flight* (Brown, N. & Taylor, J. Eds.), Louisville, KY: Sarabande Books, vii–ix.

Byrd, R. (1938/1987). *Alone*. London: Queen Anne Press.

Castaneda, R. & Klein, A. (2011). 'Flash Point Killings: Murder Most Casual.' *The Washington Post*, 11/3/2006. Retrieved 3/4/11 from http://www.washingtonpost.com/wp-dyn/content/article/2006/03/16/AR2006031602213.html

Chief Edward Moody. (2011). Retrieved 3/7/2011 from http://www.firstpeople.us/FP-Html-Wisdom/Qwatsinas.html

Chief Luther Standing Bear. (2011). Retrieved 3/7/2011 from http://www.firstpeople.us/FP-Html-Wisdom/ChiefLutherStandingBear.html

Chief Red Jacket. (2011). Retrieved 3/7/2011 from http://www.firstpeople.us/FP-Html-Wisdom/RedJacket.html

Chief Seattle. (2011). 'The Land Is Sacred to Us: Chief Seattle's Lament.' Retrieved 10/6/11 from http://home.sprynet.com/~pabco/csl.htm

Cocker, M. (1998). *Rivers of Blood, Rivers of Gold: Europe's Conflict with Tribal Peoples*. London: Cape.

Coleridge, S. (2011). 'Dejection.' Retrieved 11/8/11 from http://www.poetry-online.org/coleridge_dejection.htm

Compton, W. & Hoffman, E. (2012). *Positive Psychology: The Science of Happiness and Flourishing*. Florence, KY: Wadsworth Publishing.

Cossey, E. (2011). 'Half of teenagers want to be famous.' (2011). Retrieved 10/8/11 from http://www.parentdish.co.uk/2010/02/19/over-half-of-teenagers-want-to-be-famous/

Csikszentmihalyi, M. (1992). *Flow: The Psychology of Happiness*. London: Rider.

Csikszentmihalyi, M. (1994). *The Evolving Self: A Psychology for the Third Millennium*. London: Rider.

Daly, M. & Wilson, M. (1983). *Homicide.* New York: Aldine de Gruyer.

Davidson, R.J., Kabat-Zinn J., Schumacher J., Rosenkranz, M., Muller, D., Santorelli, S.F., Urbanowski, F., Harrington, A., Bonus, K. & Sheridan, J.F. (2003). 'Alterations in brain and immune function produced by mindfulness meditation.' *Psychosomatic Medicine,* 65(4): 564–70.

Diagnostic and Statistical Manual of Mental Disorders IV-TR, The. (2000). Arlington, VA: American Psychiatric Publishing.

Dillard, A. (1974). *Pilgrim at Tinker Creek.* New York: Harper.

Draganski, B., Gaser, C., Kempermann, G., Kuhn, G.H., Winkler, J., Büchel, C. & May, A. (2006). 'Temporal and spatial dynamics of brain structure changes during extensive learning.' *The Journal of Neuroscience,* 26 (23): 6314–6317.

Ehrenreich, B. (1996). *Blood Rights: Origins and History of the Passions of War.* New York: Metropolitan Books.

El-Zanaty, F., *et al.* (1996). *Egypt Demographic and Health Survey 1995.* Calverton, Maryland: Macro International.

Everett, D.L. (2008). *Don't Sleep, There are Snakes.* London: Profile Books.

Fordyce, M.W. (2012). *Human Happiness; Its Nature and Its Attainment.* Retrieved 1/2/12 from http://www.gethappy.net/freebook.htm

Gardiner, H., Mutter, J.D. & Kosmitzki, C. (1998). *Lives Across Cultures: Cross-Cultural Human Development.* Boston: Allyn and Bacon.

Geertz, C. (1973). *The Interpretation of Culture.* New York; Basic Books.

'Global Issues.' (2011). http://www.globalissues.org/article/26/poverty-facts-and-stats

Goldberg, S. (1973). *The Inevitability of Patriarchy.* New York: Wm Morrow.

Hall, E.T. (1984). *The Dance of Life*. New York: Anchor Press.

Hölzel, B.K., Carmody, J., Vangel, M., Congleton, C., Yerramsetti, S.M., Gard, T. & Lazar, S.W. (2011). http://www.sciencedirect. com/science/article/pii/S092549271000288X - cr0005. 'Mindfulness practice leads to increases in regional brain gray matter density.' *Psychiatry Research: Neuroimaging,* Vol. 191, Issue 1, 30 January 2011, pp.36–43.

Ingold, T., Riches, D. & Woodburn, J. (Eds.). (1988). *Hunters and Gatherers, Vol. 2.*

'Institute of Alcohol Studies – Factsheets.' (2011). Retrieved 6/7/11 from http://www.ias.org.uk/resources/factsheets/ factsheets.html

Jaishankar, K. & Haldar, D. (2011*).* 'Religious identity of the perpetrators and victims of communal violence in post-independence India.' Retrieved 6/8/11 from http://www. erces.com/journal/articles/archives/v02/v_02_04.htm

James, W. (1899/1985). *The Varieties of Religious Experience*. London: Penguin.

Jones, R.H. (2004) *Mysticism and Morality: A New Look at Old Questions*. Lanham, MD: Lexington Books.

Josephy, A.M. (1975). *The Indian Heritage of America*. London: Pelican.

Jung, C. (2002). *The Earth has a Soul: the Nature Writings of C.G. Jung*. Berkeley, CA: North Atlantic Books.

Kasser, T. *et al.,* (2004). 'Materialistic Values: Their Causes and Consequences.' In Kasser, T. & Kanner, A.D. (Eds.) (2004). *Psychology and Consumer Culture*. Washington: American Psychological Association.

Kasser, T. (2002). *The High Price of Materialism*. Cambridge, MA: MIT Press.

Killingsworth, M. A. & Gilbert, D. T. (2010). 'A wandering mind is an unhappy mind.' *Science*, 330: 932.

Kosten, T.A., Miserendino, M.J.D. & Kehoe, P. (2000). 'Enhanced acquisition of cocaine self-administration in adult rats with neonatal isolation stress experience.' *Brain Research,* 875: 44–50.

Krippner, S. (1999). 'Altered and Transitional States.' In M. A. Runco & S. R. Pritzker (Eds.). *Encyclopedia of Creativity Vol.1,* pp.59–70. San Diego: Academic Press.

Kropotkin, P. (1902/2006). *Mutual Aid – A Factor of Evolution.* Mineola, N.Y.: Dover.

Lacan, J. (1977). 'Aggressivity in Psychoanalysis.' In *Écrits: A selection,* trans., Alan Sheridan. New York: W. W. Norton.

Lally, P., van Jaarsveld, Cornelia H. M., Potts, Henry W. W. & Wardle, J. (2010). 'How are habits formed: Modelling habit formation in the real world.' *European Journal of Social Psychology,* Vol. 40, Issue 6, pp.998–1009.

Lawlor, R. (1991). *Voices of the First Day: Awakening in the Aboriginal Dreamtime.* Rochester, Vermont: Inner Traditions.

Lawrence, D.H. (1994). *The Complete Poems.* London: Penguin.

Lichter, S., Haye, K. & Kammann, R. (1980). 'Happiness through cognitive retraining.' *New Zealand Psychologist,* 9, 57–64. Also available at http://www.psychology.org.nz/cms_show_download.php?id=1044

Maitland, S. (2010). *The Book of Silence.* London: Granta.

Markus, H. & Kitayama, S. (1991). 'Culture and the self: Implications for cognition, emotion and motivations.' *Psychological Bulletin,* 98, 224–253.

Meister Eckhart. (1996). *Meister Eckhart: From Whom God Hid Nothing.* (1996) (Ed. D. O'Neal). Boston: Shambhala.

Miracle, A. W. & de Dios, Y. M. (1981). 'Time and Space in Aymara.'In *The Aymara Language in Its Social and Cultural Context,* ed. M.J. Hartman, 33–57.

Pascal, B. (1966). *Pensees.* London: Penguin.

Pinker, S. (2011). *The Better Angels of our Nature*. London: Penguin.

Pretty, J., Peacock, J., Hine, R., Sellens, M., South, N. & Griffin, M. (2007). 'Green Exercise in the UK Countryside: Effects on Health and Psychological Well-Being, and Implications for Policy and Planning.' *Journal of Environmental Planning and Management*, 50 (2): 211–231.

Radhu, N., Daskalakis, Z.J., Guglietti, C.L., Farzan, F., Barr, M.S., Arpin-Cribbie, C.A., Fitzgerald, P.B. & Ritvo, P. (2011, in press). 'Cognitive behavioral therapy-related increases in cortical inhibition in problematic perfectionists.' *Brain Stimulation*. Published online at http://www.sciencedirect.com/science/article/pii/S1935861X11000143

Raphael, B. (1984). *The Anatomy of Bereavement*. London: Hutchinson.

Ravuvu, A. (1983). *On Fijians – Vava I Taukei: The Fijian Way of Life*. Java: Institute of Pacific Studies, University of the South Pacific.

Rudgley, R. (1993). *The Alchemy of Culture*. London: British Museum Press.

Ryan, C. & Jetha, C. (2010). *Sex at Dawn: The Prehistoric Origins of Modern Sexuality*. New York: Harper Collins.

Sahlins, M. (1972). *Stone Age Economics*. New York: Aldine de Gruyter.

Schwartz, J. M., Gulliford, E. Z., Stier, J. & Thienemann, M. (2005). 'Mindful awareness and self-directed neuroplasticity: Integrating psychospiritual and biological approaches to mental health with a focus on obsessive-compulsive disorder.' In Mijares, S. G., and Khalsa, G. S. (Eds.), *The Psychospiritual Clinician's Handbook: Alternative Methods for Understanding and Treating Mental Disorders*. Binghamton, NY: Haworth Reference Press, Chapter 13.

Scott, C. (1997). 'Property, practice and Aboriginal rights among Quebec Cree hunters.' In Ingold, T., Riches, D. & Woodburn, J. (Eds.), *Hunters and Gatherers, Property, Power and Ideology*. Oxford: Berg.

Seligman, M. (2011). *Flourish: A New Understanding of Happiness and Well-Being - and How To Achieve Them*. London: Nicholas Brealey Publishing.

Solomon, S., Greenberg, J.L. & Pyszcynski, T.A. (2004). 'Lethal consumption: Death-denying materialism.' In Kasser, T. & Kanner, A.D. (Eds.), *Psychology and Consumer Culture*. Washington: American Psychological Association, 127–146.

Stewart, S.H. (1996). 'Alcohol abuse in individuals exposed to trauma: A critical review.' *Psychological Bulletin*, 120(1): 83–112.

Swain, T. (1992). 'Reinventing the Eternal: Aboriginal Spirituality and Modernity.' In Habel, N. (Ed.), *Religion and Multiculturalism in Australia*, 122–36. Adelaide: Australian Society for the Study of Religions.

Taylor, S. (2005). *The Fall*. O Books, Ropley, Hants, UK.

Turnbull, C. (1993). *The Forest People*. London: Pimlico.

Turner, A.K. (1994). 'Genetic and Hormonal Influences on Male Aggression.' In Archer, J. (Ed.), *Male Violence*. London: Routledge, pp.233–252.

van der Dennen, M.G. (1995). *The Origin of War*. Groningen: Origin Press. *Vol. 2: Property, Power and Ideology*. Oxford: Berg.

Wareing, S. (1999). 'Language and gender.' In Thomas, L. & Wareing, S. (Eds.), *Language, Society and Power*. London: Routledge.

Westen, D., Novotny, C. M. & Thompson-Brenner, H. (2004) 'The empirical status of empirically supported psychotherapies: Assumptions, findings, and reporting in controlled clinical trials.' *Psychological Bulletin*, 130 (4), 631–663.

Wildman, P. (1996). 'Dreamtime Myth: History as Future.' New Renaissance, 7(1).

Wood, J., Elaine Perunovic, W. & Lee, J. (2009). 'Positive Self-Statements: Power for Some, Peril for Others.' *Psychological Science,* 20 (7), 860–866.

Woodburn, J. (1982). 'Egalitarian Societies.' *Man,* 17, 431–51.

Woodburn, J. (2005). 'Egalitarian societies revisited.' In Widlok, T. & Wolde, G.T., (Eds.), *Property and Equality Vol. 1, Ritualisation, Sharing, Egalitarianism.* Berghahn Books: Oxford.

Wright, R. (1992). *Stolen Continents.* Boston: Houghton Mifflin.

Back to Sanity online course

For information on Steve Taylor's *Back to Sanity* online course, visit

www.stevenmtaylor.co.uk

Index

This index is in word-by-word alphabetical order.